DESIGNING THE FUTURE OF THE
SOUTH BANK

DESIGNING THE FUTURE OF THE

SOUTH BANK

A•D ACADEMY EDITIONS

PUBLISHED IN COLLABORATION WITH THE SOUTH BANK CENTRE ON THE OCCASION OF THE EXHIBITION 'SOUTH BANK 2001'

Acknowledgements

Published in collaboration with the South Bank Centre on the occasion of the exhibition 'South Bank 2001: Celebrating the Millennium – An Architectural Vision', Royal Festival Hall Galleries, South Bank Centre, London,
21st September – 6th November 1994.

Assessors for the Architectural Master Planner:
Sir Brian Corby, Chairman, South Bank Centre; Eldred Evans, Architect and Partner of Evans and Shalev, London; Anish Kapoor, Artist and Sculptor; Henry Meyric Hughes, Director of Exhibitions, South Bank Centre; Christian de Portzamparc, Architect, France; Martin Smith, South Bank Board; Nicholas Snowman, Chief Executive, South Bank Centre; Alan Stanton, Architect and Partner in Stanton-Williams Architects; Architectural Advisor: Gordon Graham
   The Strategic Brief for Master Planner Selection was prepared in March 1994 by DEGW Strategic Consulting Limited, under the direction of Dr Francis Duffy. The briefing team was led by Despina Katsikakis, with Dr Andrew Laing, Gordon McKenzie and Nicholas Zervoglos. DEGW was assisted by Jolyon Drury, of Jolyon Drury Consultancy and by Haydn Davies, of Davies Associates.

All illustrative material is courtesy of the architects unless otherwise stated.
We are grateful to Alex Ritchie, Iain Tuckett, David Hutchinson and the GLC for providing us with invaluable archive and documentary material.

COVER: View from the north bank of the South Bank Centre (photograph: Mario Bettella);
PAGE 2: Aerial photograph of the South Bank Centre and wider area, from the southwest

Editorial Offices:
42 Leinster Gardens, London W2 3AN

MANAGING EDITOR: Maggie Toy; ART EDITOR: Andrea Bettella; EDITORIAL TEAM: Natasha Robertson, Pip Vice; CHIEF DESIGNER: Mario Bettella; DESIGNER: Jan Richter

Published in Great Britain in 1994 by
ACADEMY EDITIONS 42 Leinster Gardens, London W2 3AN
an imprint of Academy Group Ltd,
a member of VCH PUBLISHING GROUP

Distributed to the trade in the USA by
ST MARTIN'S PRESS 175 Fifth Avenue, New York, NY 10010

ISBN: 1 85490 403 5

Printed and bound in Italy

Contents

DEVELOPING THE SOUTH BANK

Foreword

This publication represents the culmination of our search for an architect to master plan the development of the South Bank Centre. It has been a unique process, beginning in February this year when we issued an international invitation to architects and urbanists who wished to express interest in participating in the selection procedure for the appointment of a master planner for the regeneration of the South Bank Centre site. The announcement coincided with an exhibition at the Architecture Foundation in London, entitled, 'Building the South Bank: Architectural projects for the South Bank 1753-1993', which was shown in an expanded form in the Royal Festival Hall Galleries in May and June. Organised by the South Bank Centre in collaboration with the Director of the Architecture Foundation, Richard Burdett, and curated by Sarah Hopkins, the exhibitions provided a revealing insight into the extraordinary history of this central and increasingly important area of London.

These two exhibitions also gave us the opportunity to intensify our process of public consultation, through workshops, school projects, gallery talks and debates. The transcript of the symposium organised jointly with Academy Forum on the occasion of the spring exhibition at the Royal Festival Hall forms an essential part of this volume.

Our invitation to architects resulted in a submission from 121 practices internationally. In March, we announced a short-list of ten, and in July, three finalists were selected based on presentations made to our group of assessors. The Royal Festival Hall exhibition, 'South Bank 2001: Celebrating the Millennium – An Architectural Vision', presents each of the schemes which were developed. Together with this accompanying book they will, we hope and intend, further bring to public attention the unprecedented benefits which development in this area of the capital can generate for the nation. Crucially, we also intend them to allow informed and open debate to continue as we finalise components of the project over the coming years.

The South Bank has the potential to be transformed into the finest arts quarter in the world, with its well established world-class reputation and its unique riverside position in the heart of London. With the creation of the National Lottery and the Millennium Fund the opportunity has come to turn architectural vision into reality. Most importantly, we will bring that about by working in the closest possible partnership with our immediate artistic neighbours at the British Film Institute and the Royal National Theatre and with the wider business and residential neighbourhood as a whole, here on the South Bank and indeed across the bridges linking us to the north. The opening of the European Passenger Terminal at Waterloo will make the South Bank one of Britain's major international gateways. We are determined to play our part in making that a gateway of which we are all proud.

Our greatest debt goes to the ten architectural practices who put so much effort and thought into their proposals, each of which in its own way will enrich and stimulate the discussions to come. We have also been privileged to collaborate with Academy Group on this occasion and are grateful to John Stoddart, Maggie Toy and Edwina Sassoon for helping us to record and share this very special process. *Sir Brian Corby, Chairman to the South Bank Board, Nicholas Snowman, Chief Executive, South Bank Centre.*

EXTRACTS FROM THE DEGW STRATEGIC BRIEF

An Architectural History of the Site

The pre-history of plans for a comprehensively planned scheme of civic buildings on the South Bank goes back almost as far as the establishment of the London County Council (LCC) at County Hall.

In the inter-war period, the project of rebuilding Waterloo Bridge and the recurrence of unfruitful plans for rebuilding Hungerford Railway Bridge as a road bridge led the LCC to think in terms of a model scheme of urban planning for the area around the south end of these two bridges. These plans 'firmed up' during Herbert Morrison's term as Leader of the LCC (1934-40), when some future land purchases were agreed. This left the LCC in a position to make realisable plans for the whole area between York Road and the river downstream of County Hall as far as Waterloo Bridge.

The first scheme for the area was published by Abercombie and Forshaw in the 1943 County of London Plan. This mixed offices, shops, theatre, leisure facilities and open space. Of the arts, only theatre was included, evidently on the basis of historical associations between Shakespearean drama and the South Bank. Later, Charles Holden was commissioned by the LCC to devise a scheme for the South Bank between County Hall and Waterloo Bridge. Presented in 1948, it envisaged a national theatre and a concert hall between the two bridges, with a hotel behind. Between the rebuilt Hungerford Bridge and County Hall were to be new ministry buildings. The buildings were to be set back from the river behind a promenade; their frontages were to be determined by a line which came to be known as the Holden line.

The Holden Plan was upstaged by the decision in 1948 to hold the Festival of Britain on the South Bank. Under pressure by Herbert Morrison, who was by then a cabinet minister, Isaac Hayward, the then Leader of the LCC, agreed that they would make the whole area of the Holden plan available for the main site of the Festival, and would contribute one permanent building: the concert hall or RFH. Other structures would be cleared away at the end of the Festival, after which the area was to be developed along the lines of the Holden Plan.

The RFH was designed and built under great pressure of time. Robert Matthew, the LCC architect, was keen to ensure that the building would be in a modern style, a sign of the cultural rejuvenation of post-war Britain. Leslie Martin was appointed as his deputy, with special responsibily for the Hall and he quickly came up with the celebrated concept of the 'egg in the box'. This device, whereby the auditorium was lifted up above and within the foyer and circulation spaces, served both to insulate the auditorium from external noise and to maximise the extremely tight site. The front of the building, as originally built, was determined by the Holden line, while the back of it was set by the intention to include a smaller hall, refreshment rooms and artists' rooms. However, there was no time for both halls to be completed by 1951, so the small hall and ancillary rooms were postponed and a rear elevation was designed for the RFH by Trevor Dannatt. This pre-history of the 'small hall', the lack of facilities at the RFH and the exigencies of the Holden line are critical to understanding the later arts centre buildings.

By 1952 changes in public taste, as well as changes in government policy, meant that there was little prospect of Holden's formal plan being implemented. The County of London Development Plan of 1951 envisaged that Hungerford Railway Bridge would be retained. The Holden Plan therefore had to be radically revised.

In 1952-53 a new scheme, led by Graeme Shankland, for the County Hall to Waterloo Bridge was embarked apon by an LCC team led by Shankland. This scheme retained the deep riverside walk, but replanned the rest of the area with a mixture of freestanding buildings, interlocking quadrangles and occasional higher incidents.

It was at this stage that the belief that the RFH should not be rivalled by an equally formal building next to it took shape. The national theatre was now to be built on a site further upstream, leaving the future use of the ground between the RFH and Waterloo Bridge uncertain. On the Waterloo side of Belvedere Road the LCC planners envisaged an office block, a bus station and an air terminal. On the downstream side of Waterloo Bridge the LCC had bought thirty acres of land. Under the 1953 plan this area was to become a government science centre.

The Shankland plan was the first to consider re-planning the South Bank area to a consistent series of levels. This fashionable idea followed from the different levels of the bridges and embankment, and had been implicit in the planning of the RFH. A pedestrian walkway out of Waterloo Station to the South Bank site had also been a feature of the Festival of Britain.

A new scheme was made in 1956. The LCC had been able to find only a single taker for the high office block: Shell. The proposed bus station did not materialise, while British European Airways abandoned its projected air terminal, leaving the space between the Shell Centre and the North Block of County Hall as an underground car park for Shell. The construction of the Shell Centre meant displacing the popular 'Telekinema' – the only other feature of the Festival of Britain to survive besides the RFH. This was the origin of the National Film Theatre (NFT), which in due course was enlarged.

In 1955 the idea of the small hall tucked under and behind the RFH was revived. It was now clear that for acoustical reasons any attempt to add the small hall in the position originally intended would be unwise, because the Bakerloo Line ran closely underneath. Meanwhile the Institute of Contemporary Arts was looking for a new home with a gallery attached. This idea was taken over by the Arts Council. There was then nowhere in London, besides the Royal Academy, which could adequately house the large loan exhibitions, which were increasingly part of the international art world. Ten-thousand square feet was the initial brief for the gallery, later raised to twenty-thousand. The brief for the 'small hall' was enlarged, so that it could be used not just for concerts but also for chamber opera.

The project was to be a joint venture between the LCC and the Arts Council, using LCC architects to give the complex architectural unity. There were to be three elements: additions at the front and back of the RFH, to give it the restaurant, 'green rooms' and other facilities, together with some adjustments to the building's acoustics; a major gallery for loan exhibitions, to be run by the Arts Council; and a medium-sized, flexible concert-hall-cum-recital-room.

The internal needs of the 'small hall' and gallery were the primary concern. Acoustical consultants at the Building Research Station advised that fenestration should not be used. This influential decision proceeded from the introduction of a helicopter service along the Thames from Battersea in the late fifties, using noisy Fairey Rotodyne machines. The idea of entombing the hall in a concrete bunker and creating a 'controlled environment' for the complex followed on from this consideration. The increase of space in the gallery led the architects to return to the idea of having the buildings next to one another, but linked to the RFH at an elevated level with a terrace in front. This entailed the final jettisoning of the Holden line as a demarcation for the front of the South Bank buildings.

1960 was the year in which the South Bank buildings as they now stand were essentially designed. The special work-team consisted of Norman Engleback, John Attenborough and Bryn Jones which was reinforced with

Ron Herron and Warren Chalk from the LCC Schools Division. Experiments ensued with a wide variety of overall design solutions based on the 'controlled environment' idea, of which the most radical was to treat the whole complex as a grass-covered mound. Herron in particular made major design contributions to the exterior, while Chalk concerned himself with the walkways which were becoming a component of the scheme.

Engleback managed and co-ordinated the project and involved himself deeply with the interior of the hall and the necessary consultation with musical experts. The primary aim was to achieve an acoustic which would allow a longer reverberation time than in the RFH, and they concluded that the best results could be achieved by providing a single seating arrangement without galleries, and a comparatively large volume per audience seat, while offering some adjustability to allow for the problems of reverberant sound in the lower frequencies. At about this stage Hope Bagenal, the original acoustical consultant, gave way to Hugh Creighton, who suggested a system of Helmholtz resonators with adjustable openings lining the hall to achieve the flexibility they wanted. Meanwhile Roy Henderson, a member of the Arts Council Music Panel, had objected to an auditorium of flexible size with a possible wing which could be closed off.

A third hall, the future Purcell Room, therefore emerged in its own right. Originally planned as a rehearsal room, its potential as a small recital room was appreciated and its status raised. By another major revision, the upper part of the future Hayward Gallery was given natural toplighting.

Hubert Bennett first saw the scheme proposed for the committee late in 1960. On aesthetic grounds he was deeply unhappy with the design. He therefore worked on an alternative, somewhat in the RFH style. Faced with a committee deadline, no time or personnel to develop his scheme, Bennett backed down. Some important modifications were however agreed. Externally, pre-cast aggregate panels were to line the vertical surfaces, which had previously been wholly of bare shuttered concrete. The two auditoria and the gallery were re-planned in a rectangular relationship with one another, and the Helmholtz resonators lining the interior of the larger hall were specified to be of wood rather than concrete.

LCC committee approval was duly given to the revised scheme in 1961. WJ Appleton was introduced to monitor the building's progress. Appleton's assistant, Jimmy Blyth is generally credited with the high standards of workmanship achieved in the building. Engleback moved on to work on the first stages of Thamesmead in 1964, with the buildings barely begun on site.

The contract took over four years to complete, from 1963 till the opening of the Queen Elizabeth Hall (QEH) and Purcell Room in March 1967, and that of the Hayward

Gallery in July 1968. *(Adapted from a report by English Heritage, London.)*

An Opportunity for Rebirth

The South Bank has the most powerful concentration of arts resources in the United Kingdom. The core site and its environs already have great international cultural significance. If the visits to the Royal National Theatre and the British Film Institute facilities (the National Film Theatre and the Museum of the Moving Image) are added to those of the South Bank Centre, the total number of visits is six million per year, of which three million are attendances at ticketed events.

The site has the potential to become a great destination for tourists encompassing all aspects of art and architecture. Historically this site, which is close to the heart of London, symbolises for many Britons the hopes for a better future and a better London which were expressed so brilliantly in the buildings and activities of the 1951 Festival of Britain. However, not all those hopes have been met, despite successive improvements to the facilities on the site. Neither the core site nor its buildings, with the exception of the Royal Festival Hall (RFH), are widely enough used. The wider area has become notorious, with many homeless people sleeping rough in public spaces.

The major arts buildings on the core site have presented the South Bank Centre with logistical difficulties as the mix of performances and exhibitions shifts to follow changes in art forms and technology. Initial planning weaknesses in certain buildings have become more pronounced.

The separation of pedestrian and vehicle access onto the core site at different levels, with the use of walkways planned in the sixties, has failed to solve the problems of the orientation of the site experienced by many visitors. The walkways sterilise large areas of space beneath them and have themselves become barren. Straightforward ground level access has been made impossible.

The intention of the South Bank Centre is to preserve and transform the existing buildings, to clarify access routes to them (which may involve demolition of walkways), and to make the whole site fully accessible to the disabled.

The Millennium Fund, financed by the Government's new National Lottery, offers by 1995 a new opportunity to redress some or all of these problems, not just on the core site but also taking into account planning priorities for the wider area through joint initiatives and partnerships with neighbouring land owners and with the local planning authority. The South Bank Centre and its neighbours will also be exploring alternative public and private sources of funding.

Potential Interventions on the Core Site

The master plan must achieve the best possible relationship of the arts buildings, both existing and proposed, to each other within the core site and in relation to the wider area. The master plan for the South Bank Centre should not address the detailed briefing of any of the individual arts buildings on the site. The detailed design briefs for new buildings will form part of future design competitions or procurement processes. The RFH is a Grade I listed building. The South Bank Centre intends to restore the transparency and clarity of spatial relationships within the building as originally envisaged by its architects. Allies and Morrison Architects was appointed in 1993 to advise the South Bank Board on any alterations to the building.

In 1987 the QEH was altered to enable staged performances, such as opera and dance. This adaptation needs to be carried further to improve the technical facilities. Consultants TechPlan has prepared a plan to create a more cost effective and versatile auditorium, to improve the backstage facilities and dressing rooms and to provide a proper orchestra pit.

The Literature Section and the Hayward Gallery each need a flexible 150-200 seat venue, to include disabled seating. Uses for such a venue would include: fiction and poetry readings; small scale performance; and day conferences. A redesigned Purcell Room could serve as a venue for these activities. Improvements to the general planning of the QEH and the Purcell Room will require: improved access and foyer areas for both halls; access to the stage from outside the QEH for large instruments and scenery; dedicated escape routes for the public from the QEH.

The Hayward Gallery provides flexible and well regarded exhibition spaces but suffers from a lack of public amenities, educational facilities and storage space. There are internal environmental problems which need to be solved to meet the increasingly demanding needs of exhibitions. The Gallery requires a major transformation to provide: an extension for additional exhibitions at front of house, to allow the Gallery to remain open between exhibitions; improvements and extensions to the foyer (including introduction of a cafe, provision of lavatories for the disabled, relocation and expansion of the shop); front of house access for disabled visitors; improvements to the circulation within and between exhibition areas; provision of space for corporate entertainment and ancillary group uses; new education and public information facilities (including an orientation/audio-visual room, a visual arts education workshop, a lecture theatre, a seminar room and an information technology lab); a comprehensive overhaul and upgrade of the building's environmental systems within the galleries, storage and workshop spaces and improvements to the roof; replacements to the gallery ceilings and lighting systems; and finally, improved storage, workshop and operational areas to speed the turnaround of exhibitions and to reduce the length of closure between exhibitions.

The transformation of the Hayward Gallery may provide

FROM ABOVE: Unusable, sterilised space beneath the walkways at the South Bank; interior photograph of the RFH; the south bank as it was in the 1700s, when it was still undeveloped marsh-lands

the opportunity to relocate that part of the Arts Council Collection now stored at the Gallery. This would provide more effective operational areas for the Hayward Gallery and National Touring Exhibitions. Moreover, workshop and storage spaces at the Gallery must be extended to service the visual arts exhibition programme of the RFH.

The QEH and the Purcell Room were both designed essentially as chamber music and recital halls. Both are deficient for modern audiences. The QEH (at 900 seats) is too large for many chamber ensembles and contemporary music events, while the Purcell Room (at 360 seats) is unsatisfactory for many recitals. Given the proposed adaptations and conversions proposed for both these halls, a new auditorium is required to seat about 475 people which will be a performance hall to suit the needs of the next century. Such an auditorium will be designed technically for chamber and other musical ensembles playing the repertoire of all periods. It will also be designed to suit a wide variety of staged events. Informal and highly flexible seating arrangements are essential. The size of the auditorium is likely to be approximately 2,500-3,000sqm gross.

South of Hungerford Bridge, the Hungerford car park is part of the core site and is under the control of the South Bank Board. The site is linked to the main site area through the arches of the bridge and is the obvious prime location for a future cultural building or buildings with river and park frontage at the South Bank Centre. Once considered as the site for the national theatre, this car park has been considered as a site for a new Museum of Modern Art by the Tate Gallery. However, Shell has claimed a covenant for uninterrupted views to the river across the site. Two community groups, the Waterloo Community Development Group and the Queen's Walk Park Society have also recorded their opposition to any form of development on the site.

The arches underneath the Hungerford Bridge are owned by British Rail and have been leased to the South Bank Centre for various uses. They are positioned between the existing arts facilities and the Hungerford car park site. The use of these arches should be considered, in particular how they could be used to link the Hungerford car park/Jubilee Gardens site with the core site.

The present ground level varies but is generally in the order of +4m OD. The mean ground water level is expected to be at about Ordnance Survey Datum and will vary, with river level depending on distance from the river wall. Owing to the presence of the Northern and Bakerloo Line Underground tube-train, and a Telecom cable tunnel running underneath, any new structures requiring piled foundations over these locations will, therefore, require support locations to be co-ordinated with the tunnels. For any basements to be constructed in the vicinity of tunnels, assessment of the heave ground movements will be required prior to construction.

Based on data of past uses and construction on the site, numerous obstacles in the form of foundations and other building remnants may be expected. *(The above information on site conditions was kindly provided by Mr Tony Fitzpatrick of Ove Arup & Partners.)*

Interventions in the Wider Area
Nicholas Grimshaw and Partners have completed the Waterloo International Terminal for trains using the Channel Tunnel. The station is owned by European Passenger Services Ltd and will open during 1994. Pedestrians can gain access to the pedestrian bridges to cross York Road and reach the Shell Centre and other forms of access to the South Bank Centre. Expected numbers of passengers per day will be 24,000.

The new Jubilee Line station, to be completed in 1998 at Waterloo, will be entered from the refitted Colonnade building on Waterloo Road. The Jubilee Gardens will be temporarily used as a spoil heap for the tunnel construction.

A major consequence for master planning the area arises from the proposed relocation of the existing extensive bus and coach services using the Colonnade at the eastern side of Waterloo Station to along Waterloo Road at Tenison Way.

Shirayama Corporation with Renton Howard Wood Levin are transforming the County Hall into a hotel and entertainment/conference centre. The Council Chamber of the building will become a conference centre. Restaurants will be created along the river frontage.

The Oxo Tower is a 1930 Art Deco turret surmounting an Edwardian warehouse at Stamford Wharf. The building was derelict until it became part of a mixed-use development undertaken by Coin Street Community Builders. It will include a mixture of homes, studios and workshops, shops and restaurants as well as a tented performance area. The renamed Oxo Tower Wharf is being designed by Lifschutz Davidson. The work is currently in progress in a phased development plan.

Potential Interventions in the Wider Area
Llewelyn-Davies working with Imagination has been commissioned by the South Bank Employer Group to propose environmental improvements to the wider South Bank area. The focus is on creating an overall identity for the area and encouraging activity. An urban design framework is proposed, focusing on the riverside walkway and identifying a series of new 'places' for activities. Greater interaction between the major corporate users in the area and the public is proposed. The key areas for improvement are links between Waterloo Station, the South Bank Centre, the Royal National Theatre, Upper Ground and Belvedere Road.

P&O Development has received planning permission to develop four office buildings designed by Renton Howard Wood Levin, three along York Road replacing the existing

1960s Elizabeth House, and a fourth beside the Network Southeast terminal. The P&O Development proposal indicates further improvements to vehicle access at ground level under the new office buildings and a new pedestrian bridge at first floor level to connect the Network Southeast terminal to the other side of York Road.

Stanton-Williams has been appointed by the Royal National Theatre to advise on clarification of the main ground level entrance to the Royal National Theatre on the river front and to extend the foyers and terraces. The proposals would eliminate the road access across the river front of the building.

The NFT propose siting a wide-view screen, five-hundred seat cinema in the centre of the Bull Ring, named the IMAX Cinema. This is identified as a new gateway to the South Bank Centre, providing a link with the existing Museum of the Moving Image (MOMI) and the NFT facilities alongside and under the Waterloo Bridge. The building would be of six storeys with a raised foyer at first floor level.

Lifschutz Davidson, under commission from the South Bank Employer Group, has made proposals to improve pedestrian access from Waterloo to the South Bank. The proposal is to remove roads at the northwest of the station outside Victory Arch to create a new pedestrian piazza with ground level access to the South Bank. New coach facilities would be provided outside the International Terminal at Waterloo as well as a new bus terminus at Tenison Way. The proposal also envisages a new covered pedestrian bridge from the Waterloo East station via the new pedestrian piazza to replace the existing pedestrian crossing on Hungerford Bridge. The proposal is based on traffic studies undertaken by Ove Arup & Partners.

The existing circular road system around the station would be re-designed as a horse-shoe system, allowing priority for pedestrians in front of Victory Arch. The scheme proposes that taxis would be the only vehicles allowed to maintain a route around the station at peak times, being allowed to share the pedestrian piazza and to continue round to the International Terminal or to leave the area via the Bull Ring roundabout.

Lifschutz Davidson has also proposed replacing and extending the pedestrian walkway on the Hungerford Railway Bridge by adding a wider deck and linking it to the proposed Waterloo bus terminal and to Waterloo East. A single route is therefore achieved between Waterloo and Charing Cross without any changes of level. The bridge could have a roof that is adaptable to the weather.

An earlier proposal by Ahrends Burton and Koralek and Richard Rogers Partnership, in 1983, envisioned a Thames Centre Project to connect the South Bank with the north bank by means of a travelator linking Charing Cross to the South Bank and Waterloo. The travelator would be attached to the south side of Hungerford Bridge. The

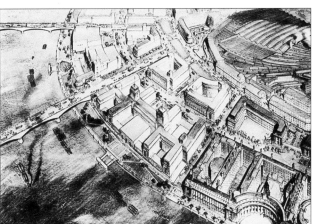

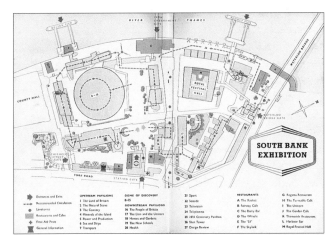

FROM ABOVE: The industrial area of the south bank, in the 1940s; plan by Charles Holden for the accommodation of 10,000 office workers on the South Bank. The buildings are set back from the river behind a promenade (David Hutchinson Collection); plan of the Festival of Britain detailing the exhibitions in each pavilion. Taken from The South Bank Exhibition: A Guide to the Story it Tells, *by Ian Cox, 1951*

scheme created improved pedestrian links between Trafalgar Square and other main areas as part of a wider project to revitalise the River Thames.

A pedestrian 'Shell Bridge' scheme was designed by Richard Horden Associates in 1989-90. The slender pedestrian-only bridge would link the South Bank Centre with Covent Garden between Waterloo Bridge and Hungerford Bridge, linking the Strand theatres directly with the RFH.

Woods River Services Ltd in 1988 proposed a new pier with two parallel jetties to be developed from the steps down to the river on the north corner of the Royal National Theatre. The pier would have provided a 160 person capacity restaurant and bar. The development was considered too large by the Royal Fine Arts Commission. More recently, John Hackshaw, a developer, has proposed a series of floating islands along the South Bank and a floating promenade along the north bank on which a variety of structures could be built, possibly forming a river development for Millennium festivities. The Port of London Authority has suggested that the existing Festival Pier could be enlarged and that a new pier could be created in front of the Royal National Theatre.

The Infrastructure of the Site

The South Bank Centre is a complex site requiring several different forms of servicing and public access. The Centre itself must service the three existing auditoria and their various activities, as well as the major exhibition spaces at the Hayward Gallery. Equally important are the needs of the NFT and the MOMI located under Waterloo Bridge, adjacent to the Royal National Theatre. The demands placed on servicing by the proposed addition of a new auditorium, an expanded Hayward Gallery, significantly higher levels of activity for retailing and catering, as well as the possibility that the Hungerford car park site may be used for a new major cultural facility, require a careful re-appraisal of existing conditions.

Deliveries number about 230 per peak day across the whole core site. Sixty of these serve the Royal National Theatre. Deliveries tend to be unstructured and intrusive. Major arts exits and entrances are co-ordinated by weekly operations meetings, but catering, retail and other arts deliveries are not controlled.

There is a multiplicity of public entrances to the arts buildings at the South Bank Centre from both lower and upper levels on the site. The RFH has five major entrances on two levels, none of which is clearly identified as the front door. The upper level entrances to the Hayward Gallery and the QEH/Purcell Room are more obviously 'front doors', but their location on the site does not make them easy to find. The problem of entrances is exacerbated by the confusion as to whether the riverside is the 'front' of the Centre even though most people walk to the site from the Waterloo side or 'back'.

The RFH is serviced from the west side parallel with Hungerford Bridge, and from a lay-by at the south immediately adjacent to the barrier access from Belvedere Road. Catering deliveries are made from the north end of the west side access road, into a corridor leading to the kitchens of the riverside cafeteria and a goods lift to the upper level. Restaurants' waste collection is via a bag compactor in a chamber adjacent to the catering entry with a daily collection. Goods vehicles turn by passing through an arch under Hungerford Bridge and run south parallel to the road on the other side to exit by passing under the bridge again at the entry barrier into Belvedere Road.

Arts deliveries to the RFH are by a goods entry at the south face leading to the only large-size goods lift with access to the stage. Orchestra pantechnicons tend to be parked in a hammerhead adjacent to the artists' entrance on the south face or under the adjacent Hungerford Bridge arch.

Goods access to the NFT and MOMI is from the access road to the west of the Royal National Theatre and east of Waterloo Bridge under which these facilities are built. The NFT restaurant facing the river is also serviced from this road.

Royal National Theatre technical deliveries are made directly from Belvedere Road, with catering deliveries at the north east corner opposite the river front: this highly visible place contains a compaction skip, stacks of empty crates and empty roll cages.

The slip road between the RFH and the Hayward Gallery is the principal goods vehicle access to the building: the Hayward Gallery dock, located on the west face of the building facing the RFH is currently the base for the South Bank Centre's exhibition transport fleet. This dock serves as a secure loading bay for incoming and outgoing exhibitions for the Hayward Gallery, National Touring Exhibitions and the Arts Council Collection. The same goods access road also serves as the entrance to the car park underneath the Hayward Gallery. Lack of storage space results in empty packing cases filling part of this loading dock area. It is difficult for trailers to enter the bay area.

Deliveries to the QEH and the Purcell Room have to be made in the 'slot' running east to west from the central access road to the core site. Goods access prevents ground-level views for pedestrians to the NFT or MOMI. The access road continues round the river front of the RFH to the east under Hungerford Bridge, and leads out through the car park to Belvedere Road adjacent to Jubilee Gardens. However, it does not connect to the RFH goods access road east of the Hungerford Bridge arches.

Car parks currently controlled by the South Bank Centre are the following: underneath the Hayward Gallery, the artists' car park on the Hungerford car park site and the public car park on the Hungerford car park site. The South Bank Centre also operates a 410 space public car park situated underneath the Royal National Theatre. These car parks provide an important source of revenue to the Centre. Demand for public parking is likely to increase.

The master plan should recommend an appropriate level of car parking on the whole site, both for existing venues and for such additions as the proposed new 475 seat auditorium and the potential major cultural facility on the Hungerford car park site. It is possible that the car park underneath the Hayward Gallery should be relocated to create more development opportunity at that site. However, Lambeth's policies on car parking provisions in this area are generally restrictive.

There have been proposals for extensive underground car parks underneath the Jubilee Gardens. The master plan must maintain the current provision of car parking for the South Bank Centre and if possible increase such provision.

Coach traffic is likely to increase proportionally and therefore appropriate dropping-off points should be proposed, as well as traffic policy enforcement measures so that coaches do not remain in the area. It should also be noted that the new European Passenger Terminal is likely to exacerbate the problem of coaches in the area, since coaches will need to use 'holding areas' in the vicinity of the terminal given that the terminal itself has inadequate coach parking provision.

Catering could provide focus and vibrancy to public spaces, benefit the surrounding business and residential community, and improve the experience of all visitors to the South Bank Centre. Retailing on the site today is essentially arts related: a book shop, a record shop and a gift shop. These shops occupy some 360 square metres of foyer space in the RFH, contributing some twenty per cent of all commercial transactions, and forty per cent of sales value. There is also a shop in the Hayward Gallery. The objective of the South Bank Centre is to expand high quality, arts-related retailing.

New retailing and catering outlets could link existing buildings or be part of the public spaces or foyers open to the public throughout the day. Contestants should also consider the potential of activities that relate to the arts activities of the South Bank Centre.

The recommended goods servicing strategy should aim to clear the centre of the core site at ground level between the RFH and the Hayward Gallery/QEH of goods servicing and any traffic penetration in order to provide the maximum opportunity for pedestrian access and to provide space for other uses. Several choices are available. For example, if the contestants wish to provide uninterrupted access to the river at ground level, the present perimeter road could be restricted to the two spurs parallel to the bridges, but notice must be taken of emergency vehicle access requirements. Regular retail and catering deliveries could be allowed to penetrate the site out of public hours and under management control. Outside these hours, goods vehicles should be confined to the perimeter zones, except for arts deliveries which need to happen all day and under secure conditions.

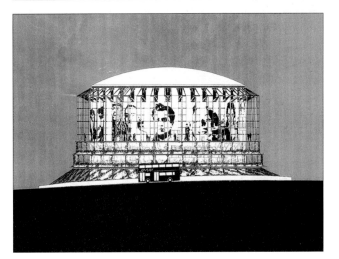

FROM ABOVE: The Dome of Discovery, during the Festival of Britain, 1951. The dome contained exhibitions on the physical and living world, the earth, the sea, the sky and outer space. It was pulled down after the Festival; aerial photograph following the clearing of the South Bank, showing the RFH, the only building to remain as a permanent structure after the Festival; elevation of the newly proposed IMAX cinema by Brian Avery Associates. It is to be sited in the centre of the Bull Ring

SOUTH BANK SYMPOSIUM
ACADEMY FORUM

Academy International Forum: The International Forum on 'Designing the Future of the South Bank' was held at the South Bank Centre, London, Thursday 2nd June 1994.

Robert Maxwell

When I was in my penultimate vacation from University, I spent the summer working for Patience Clifford designing the house and garden pavilion in the Festival of Britain – a difficult task because it involved the arrangement of some 2,500 objects into a compact space, most of them suspended on wires. Later I received a letter from Patience Clifford asking if I would like to come back and work for them – naturally I accepted and so I worked for Hugh Casson, Patience Clifford and Nevill Condor for a number of years.

The South Bank's chief success was that Hugh Casson did not attempt to impose a blanket master plan but worked to incorporate a mixture of different styles and kinds of building which would be an illustration of the architecture of views, a concept of the townscape; a concept which every body believed in except me. There are other reasons why I have particular affection for the South Bank; not only because of my involvement in 1957 with this building, for which we designed extensions at both ends which were unrealised, but also because of the six buildings I've built in London, three of them are on the South Bank.

A recent past president of the RIBA, Richard MacCormac, was part of a move to try to revalue the South Bank; to address the question of why the South Bank, so immediate to the centre of London, should be so inaccessible and so unknown? Why doesn't it look like London? Why does the South Bank and the Bull Ring look more like a part of Birmingham? This problem must be faced and a master plan must be conceived which will improve the situation. Yet we no longer have the GLC, an authority for London which would function as a mechanism to apply a master plan. All we have is a local authority. Is it possible for grand visions to exist within local authorities? To answer this question let me cite the example of the Brunel Centre which our firm built for Swindon. The town clerk was a fervent Labour follower but also a fervent patriot for his town. He chose to have a tower block built because it seemed that no development was complete without a tower block. We tried hard to dissuade him but he insisted on having a tower block. In the end it was, and is, a very nice tower block. People from any political persuasion, providing they have a sense of the locality and a wish to advance it, could, through

public debate, somehow force the hand of central government to do something out of the ordinary.

Let me pause for a moment to make the important point that this debate is entirely separate from the current competition which is in the process of selecting an architect to work for the South Bank Centre. Nevertheless this is a public issue, a matter of importance for a public debate and we are entitled as the public to debate it independently of whatever else might be happening in terms of competitions. In fact we do not yet know what the brief is, as it is not yet in the public realm; as a consequence there is no means of questioning it. If during this symposium we can pinpoint some significant issues and bring them to the forefront of the public debate, and if we can highlight factors that could effect the outcome of the competition, then this event will have been of great value.

As an admirer of the South Bank and user of the Northern Line, it seems to me that whatever string of beautiful pearls are put along the river edge, for example Sir Norman Foster's design for the NFT, still remains that prime site which could be developed with a beautiful building. But whatever happens on the sites available as part of the cultural fringe – whatever modifications may be made to make the public access to the QEH and the Purcell Room and the Hayward Gallery different – we have our cultural centre. Any additions to it are only a marginal fringe to the South Bank. The South Bank will not take off until developers see the value of it as a part of the city grid. That is my firm conviction.

Yet there is a problem here. If you look at the plan there's no question that Waterloo Station, with or without Grimshaw and the GLC, is a terrific source of the generation of public interest. But the only access is to come up along the riverside walk or from the old GLC building in Belvedere Road. In both cases you have the obstacle of Waterloo Bridge, Waterloo Station and the adjoining subway station. Up until now this has been thought about chiefly in terms of access from across the river from Westminster. There's no knowing what the City of Westminster would feel about the leakage of some of its tourist trade across the river. There's no question that a pedestrian footbridge or travelator across the river as proposed by Richard Rogers is not going to be a cheap thing to do.

I can't help feeling that whatever might be done to link it directly to the West End there's still the problem of the South Bank as a segment of London which should be made to work better. I see here a railroad of city streets that extend back from the Coin Street area all the way to the Elephant and Castle. Why don't they work better? Why aren't they more desirable for developers? There's no doubt that if one or two good buildings are built on the South Bank they could trigger a change of attitude and could act as a catalyst for development. But any plan has got to take into account the provision of access for larger numbers of people from Westminster, the proposed hotel and from the station, including people from France via the 'Chunnel'. Only when you have a hinterland with attractive retail outlets with all kinds of cafes, pubs, retail and city life, will you get the support culture needs. Only then will you have the ability to hold conferences where the dull conference lunch can be avoided, and the little restaurant around the corner can be visited. That is the kind of thing that attracts foreign visitors.

We must work to make the South Bank fully a part of the West End. This becomes all the more apparent when you consider that if you put a compass point on the Post Office Tower (Telecom Tower) and draw a one-mile radius, all this area falls inside that circle. Whatever the competition brief might produce in the way of a nice building or even a policy for the fringe, we need a vision of extending London into the South Bank area right back to the Brixton School of Building if necessary.

I would now like to introduce Alex Ritchie, of whom it need only be said that he works for Imagination and that he works with imagination.

Alex Ritchie

A lot of the buildings now on the South Bank do not address the river properly, but the 1951 Festival of Britain did that extremely well. Old photographs of the Festival show the Houses of Parliament, in the background, and in the foreground the Festival Hall with the Skylon tearing up behind. The Skylon was a wonderful sculpture. Back in 1951 London was quite flat and did not have many tall buildings. The Skylon stood out and acted as a light, as a visual beacon so people could orientate themselves towards the site.

The wonderful thing about doing the 'Festival of Britain: 40 years on' exhibition, 1991, was that it was almost like being an archaeologist. The Dome of Discovery, and about forty to forty-seven other buildings, required about a year and a half of uncovering. This was achieved either by going to visit the architects who were involved in them, or by researching some of the engineers who had worked on the buildings and put the drawings together, because a lot of the records were sadly destroyed. One interesting fact about the Dome is that you can fit four Royal Albert Halls inside it. This gives you an idea of its scale. The seaside pavilions also addressed the river. People used to come down and put knotted handkerchiefs on their heads and enjoy the water – they couldn't afford to go to the seaside so they went to the River Thames and enjoyed the sun.

15

FROM ABOVE: The Hayward Gallery; the South Bank in relation to Westminster; aerial photograph of the RFH as it is today, looking across to the north bank with Charing Cross Station in view

The back of the RFH provided shelter from the rain, which was fortuitous as 1951 was renowned for heavy rainfall. My favourite buildings are at Tinterly Street. There were eight of these pavilions rising into the sky, but there were originally meant to be nine. They were made from compressed hay, and when the horse and cart was delivering them one of the horses ate one of the cabins, hence, making them one short of nine. These were very brave pieces of architecture for their time. Maxwell Fry and Jane Drew also constructed a small pavilion that addressed the river. The Tate Gateway is one of the major entrance-way buildings coming out of Waterloo Station.

Presently, Neil Southard and I are working on an exhibition of our ideas for the millennium and they are all based on the twenty-two miles of the river, running from the East End to the West End. Close to the South Bank site we intend to put a leisure ride under the water. Instead of building more on land, we thought about putting something on the river and making it float like a barge, a series of barges that come together to create this leisure island. On the north side of the Embankment we would move the road back and have more of a promenade, so the river can be enjoyed. That is one of the nicest parts to walk in London but it is difficult to get to because it is straight and difficult to cross. Trafalgar Square, instead of being a roundabout, should become more of a public square.

The emphasis should be on moving east from the South Bank and looking at the site of the Bankside Power Station. As Robert mentioned, the 'string of pearls' should not focus on the South Bank itself, but actually go east and west. Further east to the site of the Bankside Power Station there could be a bridge across to St Paul's, and another further west towards Battersea Power Station. Once you have crossed the river you could move into north London and create a boulevard between Trafalgar Square and St Paul's, right along The Strand and Fleet Street. A recent study by Llewelyn-Davies, for the South Bank Employers' Group, included a series of gateways and four major entrances into the South Bank area. These were from Blackfriars Bridge round towards Westminster Bridge, then from Kings Reach down onto Waterloo Bridge at the water's edge, right back to the Cut where the Old Vic is situated.

The modern skyline is like a sculpture that could give directional information. In the evening it could become a light show and could act as a signing device enabling you to orientate yourself through the site. We also looked at the use of ephemeral architecture and light and movement. This was originally attempted by Misha Black, just before 1951, with the design of a fantastical master plan of the site. It is curious to note that it has many similarities to the 1851 Crystal Palace.

A project we are now working on in Atlanta for the 1996 World Olympics has many similarities to the South Bank.

It, too, is very central: the business area of downtown Atlanta is visible from the site. It has been largely forgotten even though it has a marvellous infrastructure and is very well connected. We are applying what we call 'confetti urbanism' where colour, light and movement are used to enjoy the space. The building will be a mile long. The simple thing is that it is made out of a kit of parts. It is very inexpensive to do and it stands for six months before, and six months after the Olympics.

A project we worked on with the Architectural Foundation in Croydon used the exterior of a building in the evening. At the South Bank there are a lot of flat facades which could be used for bringing the theatre from inside the buildings onto the exterior. All this is done through projection which is very inexpensive and has a wonderful effect. For the Croydon project we have proposed having balloons floating out of the buildings to attract people to see the lights of Croydon.

Nicholas Snowman

The number of people who come to the South Bank Centre, which includes the three concert halls, the Hayward Gallery and the Poetry Library, is estimated to be about three and a half million a year. However, that three and a half million becomes six million visitors if you add the National Theatre and NFT, all in a twenty-seven acre area.

The number of people who are directly employed by the South Bank Centre is three hundred of which I am the Chief Executive. In addition to that, about another three hundred people work here without permanent salaries, in other words people who sell programmes, the ushers etc. There are also the franchises and caterers that bring in services, restaurants, security and cleaning. It is a medium-sized organisation. Of a turnover of approximately £22 million, £13.33 comes from the Arts Council. Therefore, somewhere within the region of fifty-five per cent of our budget comes from this organisation and the rest we have to earn, from merchandising, box office sales, exhibitions and catalogues.

My vision is for the whole area to become a 'destination', so that people come here not simply because of the cultural activities, but because of the very environment in which those activities take place. It seems incredibly banal but actually that is the simple truth upon which we would all agree. If we could increase the number to twelve million visitors to the South Bank as a whole, that would be a reasonable aim. This depends on the brief, put together by Frank Duffy and DEGW. There is one realisation that has come to us all over the years, because there have been a lot of projects, and this is that without partnership, without our relations with Lambeth and Coin Street, IBM and Shell, this could not have happened. Somehow there has to be a creative liaison, a creative relationship between the core site which we do administer and the wider aspects which we do not. That can only work with the kind of dynamism that has already been generated by the South Bank Employers' Group; for example, by the sense of partnership that we have enjoyed with Lambeth and with Coin Street and with all our neighbours. Something has to be done about it all. It seems to me to be the big chance for London.

Geoffrey Broadbent

An important question we should ask is: how do people travel, in general, to the South Bank?

Nicholas Snowman

They arrive at the various stations, but then they have to walk into the 'rubble' through the less-than-inviting environment into which they are plunged.

Robert Maxwell

In 1957 the GLC found that eighty-three per cent of people arrived by public transport or potentially by public transport. At the walkway level we were then concerned with making the walkways work. Seventeen per cent arrived by taxi or by car at the road level. It was thought that an escalator could be supplied by BR, which would come out of Waterloo Station and be connected to the RFH.

To get to the Royal Festival Hall you still have to climb up the steps, and take a miserable walk through the forecourt of one of the dullest office buildings in London. It is not a happy trajectory. But if the route was made more attractive, you could have a majority of people arriving at the walkway level.

John Taylor

To compare the concrete architecture of the South Bank and the Bull Ring to Birmingham is actually incorrect. Birmingham, like many other cities in the region, has undergone a period of tremendous urban regeneration over the past five or six years. Present-day Birmingham is quite unlike the Birmingham of the fifties and sixties and early seventies. A great deal of work has been done in Victoria Square and there has been a lot of investment that totally transformed the quality of the urban landscape.

One of the main features which has been achieved in Birmingham, and elsewhere in the UK, which has not happened here in London, is that we now have a far greater warmth, a far greater attention to human scale. There is a quality to the environment, and also I think there is a dignity associated with some of these newer schemes which I think the public and community respond to. Therefore, cities like Birmingham have made enormous strides and provide a forum for a sort of exchange of information and ideas on a variety of urban regeneration. In terms of

FROM ABOVE: Suspended offices, Chichelely Street entrance, Architects' Co-operative Partnership, 1951; constructing the Dome of Discovery, photograph taken from the RFH; the RFH by night, with viewing platforms on the water's edge as part of the 'seaside' exhibition in the Festival of Britain, 1951

people coming into the area I would agree that there are enormous barriers which prevent them – it is very much an obstacle course.

Paul Finch

The regeneration of Birmingham was essential for commercial development if not much else. Has the effect of the cultural investment been to promote commercial schemes? Has it simply been a question of them managing to pick up economic benefits from inward investment and the exhibition centre business?

John Taylor

The successful regeneration schemes have been a combination of the physical regeneration of bricks and mortar of the hard landscape and the introduction of greater amenities, so that various cultural activities can take place. There is the social dimension and the economic dimension. The area as a whole has to be self-sustaining, otherwise what has been redeveloped gradually sinks down again. But to answer your question about Birmingham, yes I think it is quite true to say that the investment in the cultural facilities has brought life back into the inner city and that has improved the image of the city and that in itself has helped to attract urbanisation.

John Rowland

The thing to do is not to justify the cultural side of things. What underlies Birmingham's regeneration, as much as anything else, is the attention to the missing public realm. At the South Bank you work your way through the various obstacles to get to a particular place. The report which we did with Imagination sets out the broad framework of public realm in this area. It talks about and puts forward ideas about the ways of getting from point A to point B. There is no sense in having this concentration of culture on the South Bank if the area around it is 'atomised'.

An important aspect here is the community, the businesses which are around and that is what is missing, the interaction between these elements. One of the things we suggested was that businesses looked at their own particular products: what they are and what they represent. Shell does a lot of things for the environment, IBM is in computers and so forth. There are lots of things that people do here which they are not public about and which could add to the activity and character of the area by opening up something to make these companies more accessible – so making sure that you see this in terms of environmental improvement, in terms of activity, and in terms of traffic. It seems to be as important as getting the buildings right and making buildings address the environment.

If I look at the exhibition downstairs, what strikes me is the individuality, if you like, of architects coming in

and saying: 'I want a monument to myself or a monument to my particular client' and not actually looking at the wider context. It is the combination of political agendas that makes life very complicated.

I would love to do something about the Elephant and Castle; it is one of the worst places on earth. If you look at a stretch of London this would be part of the link between, let's say, Southwark Cathedral and Lambeth Palace, the two ecclesiastical points in the middle of which is a cultural centre. If we look at it in those terms then we are getting to grips with the South Bank of London; but that is just Lambeth. Westminster City Council will be very pleased to off-load some of the 'heat' that is currently in Covent Garden, where they receive eight million visitors. They would be very happy to put some of these skylons on the north bank to lead people from Covent Garden down to the South Bank. These are things that accept the idea of partnership and the idea of putting together authorities which used to rival each other.

Paul Finch

Iain Tuckett, would you like to respond to this from the point of view of a particular group of people who had a kind of ambiguous relationship with local authorities, with the GLC and with developers, over the past ten to fifteen years?

Iain Tuckett

I am going to discuss the other side of Waterloo Bridge. A lot of people think that there has been a great deal of talk about the South Bank but not a lot happening. In fact, over the past ten years an enormous amount has been happening in the South Bank area, and it is probably worth putting some of today's discussions in that context.

Almost ten years ago, Coin Street Community Builders bought thirteen acres of the South Bank, starting behind the National Theatre and including the Oxo Tower. When we bought the site it was largely derelict so we set about demolishing the buildings that were no longer required, completing the South Bank riverwalk, laying out a park and starting to build some housing. The first housing scheme was opened in 1988 – it is run by the tenants who are organised in co-ops. All of our schemes are temporary. Gabriel's Wharf was a derelict site; we have a rule that if we are not going to develop the site within a couple of years we will put it to temporary uses, like restaurants, workshops, and markets in the summer.

In 1992, having originally handed back both the riverwalk and the park to the London Residuary Body, we reclaimed the responsibility of these areas as we felt that the sort of creative management we had intended for these areas had not taken place. We have also developed the area leading from the National Theatre in front of IBM and LWT. There are some really fantastic views in this area.

Before we started work you could not see through to the river. We have our own gardening team. Last year we began a planting programme – so that it is not just the low maintenance shrubbery that is typical of public parks. We organise events and are currently building two major projects: housing in Broadwall and the Oxo Tower. The Oxo Tower is being refurbished. It will have a mix of uses, including: catering, public viewing, restaurants, five floors of housing, designer workshops and some pure retail and performance areas; this should open next spring.

The other part of our work is the partnership with the other major businesses and organisations on the South Bank. The South Bank Centre itself is one of the partners, as are IPC magazines, HM Customs and Excise, Sea Containers, LWT, Shell and Sainsbury. There are a lot of major organisations who employ about a third of Lambeth's workforce so this is a very significant part of Lambeth's economy. We have been looking at the area, and particularly the spaces between buildings which Llewelyn-Davies has mentioned.

The Shell building came at a time when the area was not considered to be very desirable, so it was built effectively to keep people inside; therefore it has its own catering, swimming pools, and shops. As a result there is no need to go out. Even though there are more people working in this area than in Covent Garden, there isn't the street life that makes the area attractive; thus shops and other forms of small business are not encouraged to open up.

Another blank area is near to LWT, but I am glad to say that LWT is considering a 'magic of TV' entrance which will introduce the public to its work. Lower Marsh, the main shopping area, is run down. We need to reverse that by getting more people moving around the area; we have got this fantastic new international terminal, but outside you can just watch people losing their way. It is a complete condemnation of the way our planning system has worked.

The South Bank Employers' Group has commissioned a couple of reports, one by Ove Arup & Partners, assisted by Lifschutz-Davidson. They came up with a number of particular proposals for improving pedestrian and traffic movement around this area. The other survey is the Llewelyn-Davies report, assisted by Imagination, which lists about thirty projects. Some are area-wide, like the signage and the gateways which emphasise the identity of the area. Other schemes are for traffic calming, improvements for pedestrians, and also the encouragement of more street life.

Another obvious area to be dealt with is the links to the north bank. This is not only on Hungerford Bridge, where Lifschutz-Davidson has proposed a scheme, but also very importantly, on Waterloo Bridge which is the main link from Covent Garden to the South Bank. The other major feature that we are anxious to encourage effectively is outdoor life. This will bring people in, and provided we manage the space, businesses will return and be viable in this area.

Paul Finch

Is it possible for conventional institutional organisations, albeit large development companies or large art organisations or government departments, to achieve the sort of incremental small-scale projects with which you have been involved? Is it possible to achieve what you've done within a broader institutional context?

Iain Tuckett

We have been responsible for planning our area, but whether it is a success or not depends very much on the businesses and other people that move into it. It is the quality of the tenants and what time they are prepared to remain open until which is absolutely essential. After we bought the site we had a lot of pressure on us by people who said: 'Why don't you run all businesses as a co-op?'. We took the position that anything done like that is never going to have the sort of life that people want. We want variety, we do not want our vision to be the all pervading vision. We want the South Bank to have its own special identity and to feel different from Covent Garden. The great advantage that we have is the fact that all of the community builders, who are the people who control the organisation, are local residents. Therefore, they know the area extremely well. We team up with large companies in the area, eg the South Bank Centre, and collectively not only can we agree on a vision for the area but the actual implementation becomes much simpler.

In fact an interesting comparison to make is with London Bridge City. There, phase one went ahead, but phase two has remained dormant. Butler's Wharf went bankrupt even though it was put into the hands of the receivers. It was a mixed development capable of a phased implementation. Now it is gradually coming to life. The importance of the approach taken by the Llewelyn-Davies and Imagination study is that it produces schemes that are capable of implementation as funds and lands come available.

Paul Finch

What are the implications for Bankside? Can Coin Street Community Builders be replicated along the river?

Iain Tuckett

I don't know whether it is healthy for a city to replicate Coin Street Community Builders! But the South Bank is a key link in the development of Central London – it is geographically directly between the West End and the City. Although both these places are on the north bank, the quickest way to walk between the two is via the South Bank. If we can then extend along the Bankside, where the Museum of Modern Art is proposing to move in, along to Butler's Wharf, then we could create a sort of loop around the centre of London which will create a very special quarter – I think Hugh Pearman calls it an *arrondissement*.

Robert Maxwell

I am very encouraged by what you say because it seems to show that much initiative on a lot of fronts is necessary to get this thing off the ground. Tradition has a tendency to think that the whole responsibility for the social scene rests on the architect. I am sure, for instance, that when Denys Lasdun was designing the National Theatre he thought that for it to be a success it had to work from the river frontage.

There is the very interesting case of the Mellon Gallery in New Haven, the gallery of British art by Louis Kahn, which was designed as an institution; but the planners of the university asked him why there could not have been a row of shops there facing the main street between his building and his art gallery. In the end, the Mellon Gallery was built with a row of shops on the sidewalk, which include a book shop that serves coffee and is a centre for student life and for life in the area. I don't think Louis Kahn was upset with the final result. By having his entrance at one end and by having the garden at the other, it maintains its own institutional life and there is no need for any conflict between institutions, and the life of commerce.

Peter Eisenman has to be named for saying that 'my building is the city – it offers the variety of the city'. This is absolute nonsense. The variety of the city is not to be achieved in any one design. It is the result of the coming together of many different things. I think when architects stop taking responsibility for the total mix, but think how they can contribute to the total mix, they make their building multifaceted by opening up to mixed use and by resolving the conflict between that use and the institutional users inside the building. They leave the whole to contribute to the neighbourhood, and we start to get into the modern city, not the modern idea of the city.

Jake Brown

I was much encouraged by Iain Tuckett's speech and also by Bob Maxwell's caution because it really fills me with alarm to see the same stories being told, which are absolutely right and yet not heeded. I do think that we are beginning to ignore some of the fundamentals of the situation, which have been created in the South Bank. The phenomenon, which we are discussing, is surely what has happened. A number of things have happened, one being that worldwide we all know and see, and probably experience, major parts of city reconstruction that dig away at the same problems, so that the vocabulary of need and accomplishment is not a mystery.

The city is changing for the first time since the Middle Ages. An idea is cautiously emerging in town halls and elsewhere that an urban area is more than the sum of parts, urban functions which traditionalists separate into waste disposal, energy, transport, pollution, health, shelter and culture. Such aspects should be linked and should be ad-dressed together, and of course that was the job that the GLC, perhaps not too marvellously, were trying to do. One thing that has not been mentioned is that by closing the GLC a major people resource was removed from this site. I worked for many years at the GLC when Lower Marsh was packed everyday with four thousand people who worked there. The place was absolutely humming with real city life. The GLC, a major city player and a significant metaphor of what should be happening in this area, was removed. I think one generally agrees with people in Davies' study and Bob Maxwell's indication that our efforts must go right back to the Elephant and Castle, to Covent Garden and to Lambeth Palace.

It becomes evident that decisive planning and political and cultural will which we do not find in this country are absolutely necessary. In Paris, the Parisians and the Government decided to restructure their underground and to embark upon *Grands Projets*. Many years ago they started on their underground. If we want to improve our underground Northern Line, and we absolutely need to if London is going to work, then we should have started twenty-five years ago. We are dealing with the fact that all of us have got to start telling those in power that the time scale in London is crucial, that there must be some sort of plan, rhythm and purpose to what we are doing.

With regard to the South Bank, there are wonderful opportunities not even mentioned in any brief, no matter how understated or non-public. At County Hall there is the opportunity for the car park to become a great space almost on a scale of the space we see in Leningrad and the two buildings, which were never really part in spirit, could easily come down and be replaced by a genuine modern building or genuine cultural purpose. Of course the London School of Economics would have allowed that. We do, however, have one remarkable building, the island block, which has been abused, but which would lend itself to transformation. It could be a wonderful traffic calmer and stop in itself. So there is a whole range of things which should be intrinsic in any discussion and which I feel are not within the power of the current exercise. One of the tragedies of this country is that wherever one's political views may lie there is a lack of will, a lack of inclination and a lack of understanding. Architecture is for everybody, not just for architects.

John Taylor

I should just like to say that I totally agree with these sentiments. It is we in London who have not got our act together. It is in London that we are not achieving the results. Manchester has put in place a strategic plan that has been developed over a period of years. But the problem is that it is not happening in London.

Paul Finch

What surprises me about the London discussions is that the two most astonishing achievements of the past five to eight years have been ignored. One example was the almost complete renewal of the City of London as a commercial centre, and the way in which the entire office life of the square mile was transformed. It is discounted now because the eighties phenomenon has disappeared. The other astonishing physical transformation which took place was of course in Docklands: four billion pounds of infrastructure and an astonishing array of new buildings and a tube line which has just begun to be built. It therefore seems to me that the idea that things do not happen in London is just not true.

In the case of the City of London it was a classic combination of fear and greed; greed obviously to make money out of real estate development. There was fear on the part of the city burghers that the city would lose its key role as a world financial city.

The Docklands are quite different. They were entirely political and were supposed to prove that you could run a purely private sector based on a regeneration exercise. It inevitably had to be bailed out and complemented by massive investment on behalf of the public purse. No Jubilee Line, no Limehouse link and no Canary Wharf. How does one break out and expand what is going on at the South Bank in a way which will produce the benign results of the development generally, in terms of economic life, in this hinterland? Is it possible that the mainspring will be the National Lottery money, which might do the landscaping, the hard paving and the Hungerford Bridge? Is that enough in itself or does it require something in addition to that? That brings us back to the question: to what extent can any kind of cultural operation or development be a catalyst for really serious urban regeneration, as opposed to simply making it more pleasant for the people who work there and the people who are involved in the hinterland?

Geoffrey Broadbent

I think another thing that it needs is proper routes up and down the river. I first came to the South Bank in 1951 and I thought it was wonderful; I could go to Battersea on the boat and various other places. I went to Venice and thought that the two cities were doing the same thing, but of course they are not. London has changed a great deal, the riverboats are not so good as they used to be. Nevertheless, as a provincial I find it extremely pleasant to arrive at Waterloo, pass by the RFH and spend the day visiting the Tate or the Design Museum, or the river at the South Bank.

David Dunster

I suppose my relationship with the South Bank is not quite as old as Bob Maxwell's, but I may be one of the few people who have actually worked on the QEH, because I

FROM ABOVE: The Skylon from the Festival of Britain, 1951; proposed extention to the Hayward Gallery by Feary & Heron Architects

did carry lumps of wood there when I was a student. I have just taken up a job at South Bank University, and one of the things that concerns me about this meeting, is that it should be looking not to answer questions but to set an agenda. What would be on that agenda? Many of the speakers talked about this side of the river as if it were a cultural strip belonging to the north side – does it belong to Westminster, Whitehall and Covent Garden or does it belong to the river? I think that has to be on the agenda. I am also concerned that the provincial Geoffrey Broadbent would come up to the South Bank and simply stay around this area, because in the six months I have been coming down the Wandsworth Road I have found it to be quite extraordinary, a great place to explore.

The second thing is that this side of the river has an advantage which the north side does not have, and that is that it does not have an Embankment road. Now that Embankment road, whether it is modelled on Paris, or Paris is modelled on it, is a disaster because it cuts the city off from the river. So the opportunity on the agenda here is to connect London to the river, and that is unique to the South.

The third thing on the agenda, for me, comes from Bob Maxwell's story in his introduction about how there was to be an escalator coming out of Waterloo Station and connecting towards the Festival Hall. Now, how many times has one heard architects discuss a scheme which has not worked, because something has gone wrong with the planting of the hard paving or, in this case, the strategic developments? This suggests to me that what perhaps should be on the agenda is a larger question and that is not to think about the surface of the earth as if it is water or hard paving on which you have benches for the homeless to lie. We must think, instead, of the surface of the land as something that a master plan must tackle. Who, for example, decides on the width of pavings? One of the significant differentiations between London and Paris is the width of pavings. What I hope to see coming out of this discussion is a substantive agenda about who decides what our city looks like. In many ways this reinforces John Rowland's point about the public realm. I have slight difficulty with the term 'public realm' because I also want people to be slightly naughty and normal.

One of the things that should be on the agenda is whether this is very specifically a north London site or whether it is the more obvious area which certainly goes with the Elephant and Castle beyond Whitehall. This must be to do with who controls the surface that people walk on and how those surfaces can be dealt with.

David Hutchinson

This is a very complex issue. There have been moments when a grand plan, the building of infrastructure, has been put forward, adopted by a city and financed by industry.

The conventional wisdom in this country is that infrastructure rose and is controlled by national government. By and large, I think that is still the case in London. What I would suggest, however, is that this need not be the case, certainly with respect to the amount of money which a road building programme costs as opposed to the amount of money a building costs.

Paul Finch

What about the funding of cultural development and its relationship to its hinterland? Is it the same story for Carnegie and how it makes money, ie by setting up a foundation to be popular and unloading the cultural facility in the middle of a poor area, because that is where the land is cheap and where everybody walks away?

David Hutchinson

Well, it varies enormously. In Chicago, and the Burnham plan in so far as it was carried out, it was very significant to be made part of the large park plan.

John Rowland

I think it is very interesting when you talk about losing control. We have reached a point when we can simply look at what has happened, when to a certain extent people have to lose control, where our environment has been dispersed by pressure from territorialisation. We are also looking at partnership between funding and professions and this is what urban design is all about. Urban design starts playing a part because it seems to be a vehicle to bring together the community and professions and create an agreed series of agendas.

Paul Finch

If someone waved a magic wand and said 'there is your employers' group plan, here is the funding to do it', who would be the client? Is there a body which is capable of presenting that to the Department of Transport, to the local authorities and to whoever needs to be consulted?

Iain Tuckett

The answer is that the South Bank Employers' Group did agree at the last meeting to set up a formal body and then seek to go into partnership with the two local authorities. The purpose of this South Bank partnership is not necessarily to carry out all of the work but to co-ordinate a lot of the initiatives and then to ensure that they are properly followed up in terms of management. However, that does not mean that the body will play any other role, ie being the conduit for money or a co-ordinator of Coin Street like the South Bank Centre (who already undertakes large amounts of the management responsibilities in this area).

Paul Finch

Kate Heron, architect, planner and member of the South Bank Group, has been involved with counter-propositions to the rather grandiose cultural post-modernism, which some fear was being presented in the last Stuart Lipton/Terry Farrell scheme. Alternative proposals were of a low cost, low incremental nature. Clearly, things have moved on since then, probably for the better.

Kate Heron

I think we reached a very interesting point in the first half of this symposium when we started talking about contributing to the public debate. It seemed that we were addressing what can be achieved for the public. Two clear points have arisen. First was the solution of incrementalism as a way of planning in which you have a list of projects that are all achievable and are within a common aim. Therefore you have a collection of people who have a common aim that has caused them to come together, although they may be very disparate in their parts. The second thing, which was quite breathtaking, was that the South Bank Employers' Group set up a body which could achieve some of these increments. That is quite new for this area, although the Coin Street Builders have already achieved a great deal. How the increments might be achieved needs to be thought about.

I've been part of something called the South Bank Group which was started about three years ago by Trevor Dannatt and Judith Strong. Its purpose was specifically to oppose the previous master plan here at the South Bank. Originally the argument was to keep existing buildings and repair them, sometimes make minor improvements and additions, but essentially to respect the existing architecture and add to it. That stage has gone and we are now several stages further ahead, but the South Bank Group sees a role for continuing its pressure and contributing to the briefing session that DEGW organised. This has culminated in the brief that the pre-finalists are working on at the moment. The South Bank Group sees itself as continuing to monitor and lobby. It is quintessentially a quiet, organised group and very much welcomes new members. People come and go as issues affect them or when they can do something in particular. What I would like to suggest is that members of the public can change things greatly and I think that is beginning to happen at the South Bank Centre. Its environment is actually an example of that. So I am suggesting that this notion of incrementalism is actually completely contrary to the notion of master planning.

I am an architect who has a very particular interest in certain buildings. I am an architect who has a particular interest in the arts. I am an architect and not simply a member of the public and I have a very strong feeling that members of the public should take responsibility for areas that belong to the public, areas of public amenity. People should also ask about public funding. We know that public areas are not going to be funded in the way that they once were, directly from the public purse but what is the balance between these things? How are they determined? How are the people that provide the money able to seek answers from the people that they give it to? There is a complicated issue of answerability and responsibility – who looks after that public territory, who decides how that public space is serviced? As David Dunster pointed out, it may be the quality of the surface of the ground that you are walking on that may make you feel that you are in a place that you can linger in or in a place that you're very unwelcome. At the South Bank Centre the ground outside the buildings is publicly owned by virtue of the Arts Council, in its original lease to the South Bank Centre. If we think about other public spaces in London, like Broadgate or Cabot Square in front of Canary Wharf, they are privately owned public spaces and are privately run and privately policed.

Perhaps the thing to end on is this notion of the relationship between commerce and culture and that each is seeking the other in order to generate more of itself. Here at the South Bank Centre there is something that has occasionally been called a culture ghetto and it is seeking the commercial influx that will give it a wider range of public which, in turn, will cause more people to come here. From the figures that Nicholas Snowman gave earlier, the aim is to actually double the number of people attending the South Bank Centre.

However, there are other areas where local authorities are expecting culture to promote commerce, and I have in mind two quite clear examples that I have worked with. One is St Ives in Cornwall where commercial prospects have been improved. The other is in Southwark where Southwark Council is very happy that the Tate will be going to Bankside and sees it as a way of generating commercial interest in that part of London. So there are paradoxes. I suggest that the public debate is only part of it, and much can be achieved if they do a little more than just debate it.

Paul Finch

The South Bank Centre is an entirely municipal creation of a sort which Birmingham has embarked on in recent years, but which in London has apparently become almost impossible. The reason for the development of places such as Broadgate and Cabot Square and the private companies controlling them is the view that local authorities are either uninterested or incapable of doing this and that it represents a new form of public realm since these new places are publicly accessible. You do not need a ticket to get into Broadgate even if it is Securicor monitoring it rather than the nonexistent Metropolitan Police.

What seems to be happening in relation to the proposals

for the expansion of the South Bank Centre is this interesting idea of a combination, not of developers and commerce who will insert commercial elements into the cultural side in order to provide the finance to produce extra facilities, but commerce in the form of local employers. What is more they will not act like Stanhope, by doing deals with the local authority. At Broadgate you get planning permission with a deal for the local authorities to raise money to build swimming pools or whatever they want to do. Every square foot of office space is given permission. But what has been talked about here is a quite different proposition, a group of interested but not owning parties in a kind of development sense. The South Bank Partnership is a joining of forces with the local authorities – but I wonder whether anybody thinks that this is likely to work.

Take Lambeth Council, for example, and until quite recently Southwark, and look at the net contribution to the regeneration of the hinterland of the South Bank Centre. Just look around the nonexistent Lambeth Council; it is notorious for being incompetent and has produced very little of added cultural value to the area for years. Southwark seems to have changed its spots, but until quite recently Southwark's major contribution to the South Bank Development was not to have any local plan for north Southwark. It was taken by surprise when somebody suggested it might like to put ten million square feet of offices up – it answered that it hadn't got a local plan for it. It has been pointed out that since the war Southwark have had to think about producing one. Perhaps it is time they did. Furthermore, it actually opposed on planning grounds the reconstruction of the Globe Theatre, a piece of madness which is unusual even for London. Happily, it seems to be behind them but I am wondering if anybody feels either optimistic about this sort of partnership or thinks that it is stepping into a new sort of unknown. Michael Compton, do you have any view about Lambeth and the general development of cultural facilities?

Michael Compton

I do not want to talk about Lambeth because I would probably get all my facts wrong. However, I should like to say two things. I am, in principle, in favour of an incremental scheme taken in a general sense. Having said that, I would hope that increments would allow plainly disastrous buildings to be pulled down, particularly the Hayward Gallery. This is a building where the people who were eventually going to use it, principally the Arts Council, were not allowed any input into the brief for the building. It was not until a late stage that they were allowed to see the architects' proposals. At some point some years before the building was opened it was decided that it would specialise in art exhibitions rather than the miscellany of amateur exhibitions, photographers' exhibitions, industrial

exhibitions and so on, for which it had originally been designed. However, the result is a building for fine art exhibitions. It is probably the most stupid in the world and I would hope that some of the buildings on the site are reconsidered.

There is the rather Utopian thought that what may be done on the South Bank site will have huge effects on the urban ambience going back to the Elephant and Castle. I hope that the people who work on the brief, the architects and everybody else involved, will keep their noses fairly close to the grindstone and think about how the individual elements of the South Bank are going to work. Also I hope they are going to think about the kind of people who in fact use these facilities. For better or for worse, this is mainly the highly educated middle classes. The experience of the Pompidou Centre should be noted, which is probably the most successful arts centre considered statistically or numerically in the postwar period. Something like eighty per cent of the people who regularly go to the library, of the eight or nine million annual visitors, do not even know where the Museum of Modern Art is. It seems extraordinary considering it is only two floors up. It is true that the building has been carefully designed to give wonderful views of Paris, for which it is rightly celebrated, but it gives extraordinarily bad views of the entrances to its own facilities. The glass frontage is of absolutely no use to the Museum of Modern Art. Considering that it is the first or second best collection in the world its attendance is approximately a million-and-a-quarter visitors, in spite of the eight or nine million who go to the Pompidou Centre and a probable fifty million who go the whole regenerated area of the Les Halles and the Marais.

In the four years after the Pompidou Centre opened, there sprang up many of the avant-garde or most active galleries in Paris in the area of the Beaubourg. They put on exhibitions of mainly contemporary art from all over the world. These galleries have slowly disappeared from the immediate neighbourhood; it seems they do extraordinarily little business. They have moved further away in the Marais so that they are actually no longer on the same public transport conduits that bring people in masses to the Beaubourg.

Finally, I should say that most of the people here seem to be concerned with town planning. Urban redevelopment can occur but the one thing which allows this phenomenon of a group of cultural institutions to grow and flourish is low cost, low rent buildings, shops and restaurants. I am worried that the sort of grandiose redevelopments that seem to be in the mind of at least some people here would have the effect of putting rents up, and there would be too much new housing, new shops and so on. The only people who could exploit these would be those selling enormous numbers of printed T-shirts.

Jeremy Melvin

My first point, given that I have lived on both sides of the river, is that there are some things which are very similar about both sides. In particular, the characters of a place like Lower Marsh where there is a market and a few rather shabby shops, and somewhere like Stratton Ground off Victoria Street which is really quite similar. I would also like to pick up on the criticism of Lower Marsh. Since the GLC has closed, Lower Marsh has become a slightly less depressing shopping area.

My second point is that there is a curious anomaly in the planning of London. Like Dresden, it is actually built on the outside of the bend in the river; it would for defensive reasons, perhaps a thousand years ago, have been more logical to build it on the south bank where the river would have formed better natural defences. The reason for that is that this bank was very marshy and much more prone to flooding than the north bank and consequently it would not have been feasible. I also suspect that the fence was never quite as important a factor in London as it was in some cities on the continent. As a result we have a curious anomaly where geographically you would expect the true centre of London to be at the South Bank, whereas the centre is elongated between Westminster and the City.

My third point is if it really is the shortest distance, as the crow flies, between the West End and the City to go via the South Bank, why then do London Transport not run a bus route along there? There is no single bus route that crosses the river twice. London Transport might be prevailed upon to recognise that geographical fact.

Paul Finch

Kate Heron, perhaps you would like to respond to the attack on the Hayward Gallery, and perhaps its incremental demolition – is there a place for demolition in your scheme of things? Then perhaps somebody might like to comment on Michael's point that the concentrated effort in relation to this master plan should be about what happens to the South Bank Centre; and that considerations about addressing the wider hinterland are either Utopian or, if the example of Paris is true, pretty much doomed to failure.

Kate Heron

I should like to defend the Hayward Gallery. I think that it has put on some of the best exhibitions one is likely to see. And what works very well about that building is that it has been able to put on exhibitions of a very different nature. It would seem to be one of the most flexible buildings I can think of, and in fact the flexibility of internal division has proved to be quite surprising. I think it was a carefully thought out building of its period and that it should be retained, although it needs work doing to it to make it more useable. However, I think the main gallery spaces are good

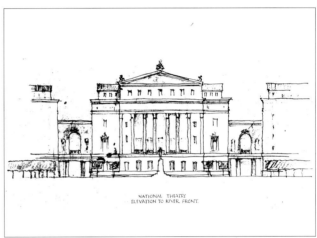

NATIONAL THEATRE
ELEVATION TO RIVER FRONT

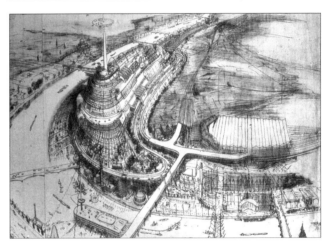

Alternative proposals which have not been realised. FROM ABOVE: A scheme by Clive Entwistle, 1949, published in Architectural Review; *proposal for the National Theatre by J Herbert Worthington in the 1940s. Worthington was appointed as consultant following the death of Sir Edwin Lutyens; the first concept for the use of the South Bank as the site of the Festival of Britain, by Misha Black, drawing by Hilton Wright. Published in* The Ambassador, *August 1946*

gallery spaces. The area can be almost doubled by using and reusing spaces.

Henry Meyric Hughes

I ought to say something in defence of the Hayward. It is not a building whose presence you can deny. What is exciting is that the building is the home of temporary exhibitions. It is not a museum. With a museum you return to find friends and seize the images that you remember on the walls, whereas a temporary exhibition space can be quite disturbing. I therefore argue in favour of the fundamental spaces and interesting geometry of the building's exterior. The ceiling and the roof need to be completely reviewed, to put it charitably, the lighting needs to be overhauled.

I think the object of the exercise would be not to transform the physical appearance of the Hayward but to add all the public amenities that were never thought of, such as the educational spaces and public circulation areas. I am thankful we have removed the little cafe which spoiled that space at the top of the building, but we need a cafe, somewhere people can meet and talk, and we also need a proper book shop which does not reach into the Gallery space. In fact we need to colonise at least the ground floor and possibly some of the surrounding areas just to bring life to the building and to break out of its bunker-like aspect. I believe it was designed to be a bunker because of the noise and disturbance of the rotor service which ran up and down the Thames at the time. What we want to do is to open up the Hayward Gallery — make it somewhere more pleasant to visit.

Robert Maxwell

When I was working on the RFH extension the excitement wasto do with a transformation of the urban scene, by means of the raised walkway which was to be the principal approach. We did our own research to show how useful it would be as an approach to the RFH. It would have led to an approach at the upper level on the landward side where you entered under a canopy with steps up from the taxi rank and come straight into the RFH onto the overhang of the box. You would then pass straight across with a space opening up towards you and with staircases ahead. That vision faded but it was part of the vision for a new pedestrian world in which we would be free from traffic, a vision shared by everybody at the time.

We still like to walk in areas that are protected against traffic, and it is not so much a question of banning traffic but trying to find a more judicious balance of traffic. I think the combination of spaces is what is wonderful about big cities. Too rigorous a division and too rational a programme writes out all those accidents that are essential for city life. The Hayward Gallery is just one incident among many

important incidents. It may be important in its time but it is not the key to the problem we are facing as a whole. Just as the RFH was built without sufficient space for the restaurant and without changing accommodation, the Hayward Gallery needs additional facilities. One can retain the Hayward, I am convinced, with changes to the walkway system — not necessarily to abandon the walkways entirely but to incorporate features from them by having a skateboarding area down under. What seems to be important is the general approach to the area and incrementalism and the ability to make a strategic decision.

John Welsh

It seems extraordinary that yet again we are bringing together the architectural establishment of the country, the big names, that get involved in every single project in the area. Their commitment to architecture has never been questioned at any point, it has just been presumed that somehow they have something of value to contribute. What about talking about cultural establishments and people rather than business? We brought up the subject of Paris, which everyone does, and it is extraordinary that we are finally trying to bring about these grand projects, fifteen years after Paris. France seems to have become rather tired of it because what you have in Paris is a lot of big, rather ugly buildings put up by mediocre architects. Not only has it happened in Paris but it is also a virus that has spread throughout France. Every little *mairie* with a lack of confidence has decided to put up a congress centre and huge tower block with no reason, whatsoever, for it being built, apart from satisfying egos. It seems rather sad that Britain is now doing the same.

Britain, however, is doing it the other way around because we started with Birmingham by putting up mediocre buildings, rather than starting in London. We seem to be going into this without thinking about social dimensions. We have talked about the aesthetic problem in that it might be turned into Covent Garden, but how do we ensure that it becomes more than just a cultural ghetto? How do we make it a part of the public domain? The public is *everyone;* it is not just the people who come to the South Bank Centre. I think perhaps we ought to look to somewhere like Holland where the established architects have been looking at social housing as well as cultural establishments and therefore reviving the city in an entirely different way to that of France.

David Dunster

Maybe there is an interesting generic problem, without getting idealistic or Utopian, which is: what does the city actually do when it is faced with a redevelopment problem where the sites are in such enormous unified ownership? What slightly worries me about the incrementalist approach, and John Welsh's comments, is that if the Pompidou has produced a sleaze bucket, isn't that rather good? All cities need sleaze. There is a more interesting agenda which has to do with looking at the possibility of an urban development here which is both good and bad and I do not mean ugly by bad – I mean sleazy.

Paul Finch

When Prince Charles complained about the National Theatre looking like a nuclear power station he did not make any explicit reference to either Battersea Power Station or Bankside Power Station, within whose purlieus the National Theatre might be said to stand. I never thought of it as a contextual building in quite that way before.

Julia Rowntree

I am from LIFT which is the London International Festival of Theatre. We have recently organised a seminar with the ICA and a range of artists which includes a younger generation of directors like Deborah Warner, Stephen Daldry and the leading carnival designer Clary Salandi as well as various other contemporary performance artists.

One of the issues that we faced staging events from all over the world in London, over the last thirteen years, is the lack of a flexible, mid-scale venue. Many of the artists that we commission, who don't come from a white mainstream culture, feel completely uninspired by the existing auditoria, ie the QEH which really is a concert hall. Although the programming is varied there, fantastic scope exists for a venue of that size to present contemporary work.

To return to the sleaze factor, I often think that what inspires contemporary artists is the transitory character of a flexible venue; a venue which isn't going to be suddenly over-burdened with enormous high-tech provision. Indeed there are many artists who are working in found space because that is apart from the burden of the cultural flagship.

In all arguments about urban design and buildings inevitably there is an emphasis on buildings, and it is a great challenge to deal with specific artistic inspiration when one is dealing with such a massive conglomeration of art forms, as with the South Bank Centre. A great deal of planning should go into how the outdoor spaces relate to the indoor spaces in terms of the possibility of programming work which isn't white mainstream culture, going right the way through to customer care and the culture of numbering seats. I was at an Ethiopian concert at the QEH recently when the culture of paying homage to the musicians on stage, by the most venerable members of the audience, was rapidly put to an end due to fears of a fire hazard.

Henry Meyric Hughes

At the moment we're in the middle of a competition for a master planner. We haven't yet got down to talking about buildings precisely. We keep talking about functions and

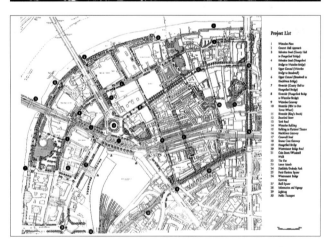

FROM ABOVE: Model of Lifschutz Davidson's proposal for a new pedestrian bridge to replace the existing makeshift structure as part of its proposals to improve circulation at Waterloo; the South Bank symposium held by the Academy Forum on the 2nd June, 1994; the South Bank environmental improvement project by Llewelyn-Davies/ Imagination, listing thirty projects

are extremely aware of the need to cater for a much wider variety of functions and audiences than ever before. Part of the brief will be to construct a flexible auditorium which will accommodate a variety of activities. It is a twenty-seven acre site. I hope that we already use the space constructively and imaginatively. Also, the Hayward Gallery aims to construct an additional exhibiting space which will be much more accessible. There will be no entrance fee, and there will be activity outside the main exhibition seasons.

Gerry Carter

If you look at the places that used to be in London before you had Earl's Court there was a lovely triangular site. Here there were all sorts of Wild West shows, rodeos and empire shows. But eventually a horrible concrete building was built in its place. The South Bank must learn from this and not make the same mistake. Instead, why not use temporary structures that could be taken down and tour the world?

Robert Maxwell

The South Bank Centre is the nearest thing to the Pompidou Centre that we have in this country. This is because the building was meant to have floors which changed level according to need. That proved to be too expensive and full of unsolvable problems. It was therefore built in a sense of compromise. There are all sorts of interesting drawings which show the outside as a kind of walking billboard, but the built project ended up as just the walking escalator. This illustrates the difficulty of building something which is meant to be a vision of the future. We cannot build an entirely alternative city – it is logistically impossible. Le Corbusier's city for two million was an instant city – he didn't even attempt to discuss the logistics of obtaining it. The population of Milton Keynes after twenty years is two hundred thousand and it has already developed and has a history.

Port Grimaud is a similar case, though rather more successful because the developer only had to simulate the growth of the city. Naturally he put the high-rise blocks on the edge of the city – where they would have been built if the city had developed naturally over time. I always remember Peter Smithson's comment: 'Port Grimaud is acceptable because it used the street system with which people were familiar and it was done with picturesque effect'. Admittedly it was a false city built for rich, retired people but it was an interesting experiment. Originally Peter and Alison Smithson had attempted to design a city completely segregated by decks running on different levels. Pedestrians would be separate from the traffic running on the ground level below. Amongst my generation, Peter Smithson tried hardest to bring in a new vision of architecture, and fell furthest when the vision proved to be impractical.

If the street has turned out to be triumphant, and not capitalism, then I think we have to accept that. This was

behind the Terry Farrell scheme to bring everything back down to ground level around the RFH, which to an extent I would agree with, but not to the extent of completely ruining the Hayward Gallery. The Hayward Gallery has to be improved but not to the extent of sacrificing it. Nevertheless the Hayward Gallery is part of the public walkway system and it's not a jewel that can be effectively isolated. If you are of the opinion that it is an historic building and it therefore must be preserved then you've raised a very difficult issue. In a sense 'jewels' cannot be changed. Currently we have proposals to change the National Theatre. This is an example of a building which needs to evolve to accommodate a changing brief. That was what modernity was all about: flexibility and response.

Today we have learned about the incremental approach and about its danger; insofar as it may fail to meet a crisis. For example, it may avoid making a good decision about the Hayward at an early enough stage. The incremental approach is what has always worked best in small communities, work with the status quo. However, this approach doesn't necessarily make that leap in time which Smithson called for to meet a new demand or situation. Therefore both the incremental approach and more visionary approach must be adopted. We should avoid taking sides. It's not the case that high tech and classical revival are the only possibilities. Modern architecture will develop according to the existence of the programme – that's what it was invented to do, to be flexible. We have to be prepared both to preserve the principles that were good and meet the needs of new conditions.

John Welsh has raised this question of the people. I would like to hear Jake Brown's comments on what happened to the people who inhabited Covent Garden before it was turned over to the tourist trade. I seem to remember that they were mostly shop keepers of the type whom Marx categorised as the most reactionary bourgeois minds in existence, so there was a paradox in that Brian Hanson struggled to fight for these people. The question then is: what rights do the people in Lambeth and Southwark have? Are they faced with an invasion of the middle class? It reminds me of Maurice Culot's not entirely successful bid to defend Brussels twenty years ago against British business men building high-rise blocks. There are paradoxes about changing territory which one must recognise. Was it the American author, Hirsch, who said 'Television sets. I own one but I don't in any way inhibit your owning one. But a villa, I own a villa in that place and that inhibits you owning a villa in that place'.

There is a difference between real estate and the terrain which belongs to everybody. In the case of a capital city like London, the people don't have a right to it because it's a capital city and it therefore belongs to the nation. The answers to the paradoxes are not at all clear. We don't know how to plan cities, the art of urbanism has never properly existed. Le Corbusier's city for two million was a hoax – it was a complete fantasy. Friedman's idea for recreating Paris in steel above the real Paris was an illusion. We have a very difficult problem here. But if the South Bank could focus public concern on what would be good and useable, this would have a galvanic effect on our culture. We're worried about lagging behind the French, but I've been to Paris to check out the *Grands Projets* and I agree with what was said about most of them being secondary projects by secondary architects. Having said that, there are things that we can learn from the French. The Paris underground runs on rubber wheels, virtually noiselessly, and it is greatly superior to ours.

The real danger about the development of the South Bank is not so much that it would cause an invasion of the 'chattering classes', driving the local population into Kent looking for David Dunster's birthplace; the danger would be that we can't ever again achieve the same high-level public interest that would get something big off the ground. There's a long way to go before this sector of London is fully developed and finished. It will be a part of an incomplete city for many more years and during that time there will be a frontage of land values – the Elephant and Castle will be at the bottom of the land value pile for a long time. All the ancillary uses that we enjoy, including the 'sleaze' factor will be able to survive. These 'sleaze' factors, like the corner shop we used to have in housing estates, will now survive the new rent levels, the new exploitation and the new clean accountancy.

Therefore we also have to accept that development is a mixed blessing and doesn't bring a final situation of paradise. It's only a process which allows values to change rather like the way weeds run into a garden. If we can get the momentum with the aid of all the people we heard today, some of whom have had marvellous suggestions to offer, we could reach a point where it tips the balance and a development starts to happen on its own and at that point you don't need a master plan. At that point the values will start working through the planning grid; and if the day ever comes when the Elephant and Castle is transformed, I hope to be alive to see it.

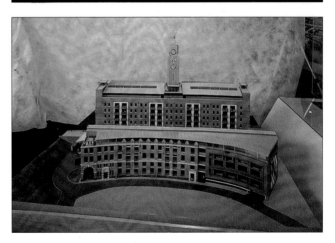

The wider area. FROM ABOVE: Waterloo International Terminal, by Nicholas Grimshaw and Partners; Coin Street Community Builders organise a programme of outdoor activities; model of the Oxo Tower Wharf mixed use development, by Lifschutz Davidson

THE PRE-FINALISTS
ALLIES AND MORRISON ARCHITECTS

There are three principal goals which this new master plan seeks to achieve. The first is to reintegrate the South Bank Centre with the city that surrounds it; for a variety of historical reasons the Centre has remained isolated from its immediate surroundings, with its relationship to Belvedere Road in particular confused by a maze of service routes and high-level walkways. The aim here has been to simplify these relationships, and to ensure the full assimilation of the Centre within its wider context.

The second is to make the best possible use of the existing buildings on the site. The brief for the competition presumes that the main public spaces of the Queen Elizabeth Hall and the Hayward Gallery should be incorporated into any new proposals. Allies and Morrison have aimed to prove that such an approach has the potential to encourage a strong architectural solution.

The third goal is to provide the South Bank Centre with a strong sense of unity. Today the Centre exists as a disparate group of buildings, united only by the structure, and the aspirations, of its management. Particular importance must be placed on the need to transform the relationship between the individual buildings in order to accommodate and represent the important links between the different activities on the site.

A Sense of Unity
At present, links between the buildings are provided in the form of the free-standing concrete walkways which bridge the service roads below. Since these walkways are carelessly planned and ill-served by narrow, dogleg staircases they would be removed. Their legacy, however, would be a group of buildings whose public foyers are all planned at first floor level.

30

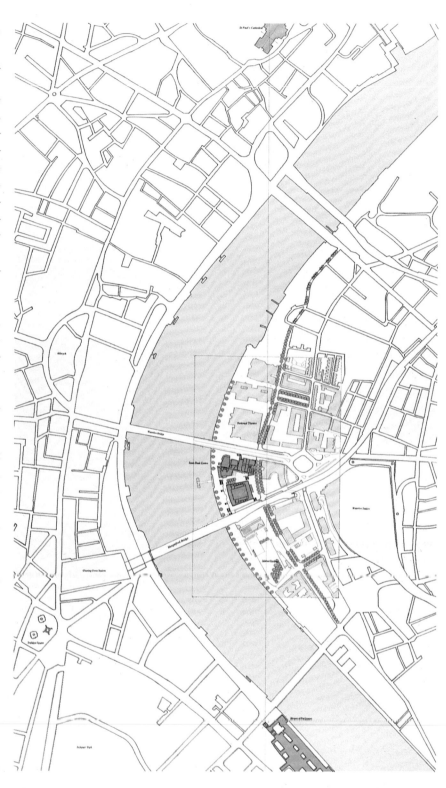

South Bank site plan; OPPOSITE ABOVE AND BELOW: Mezzanine; ground floor plan

Rather than working against this defining characteristic of the site, it is proposed to replace the walkways with an uninterrupted pedestrian podium, or *piano nobile*, extending the full width of the site. Approached by generous staircases from Belvedere Road and the river walk, the podium would allow direct connections between the buildings on the site. At podium level the connection would take the form of a major new public space. At ground level it would be an enclosed shared foyer, containing cloakroom and toilet accommodation as well as retail facilities, and providing access to each of the buildings.

Within the foyer of the Royal Festival Hall (level 2), the effect would be to extend the visual transparency of the building into a physical permeability. Visitors to the RFH would be able to walk directly from the foyer across an external space to the relocated Hayward Gallery entrance, an arrangement which would also be available below the podium to allow a sheltered route.

The new external space would be the heart of the South Bank Centre, a great vestibule leading to, and overlooked by, each of the individual buildings. Located at first floor, rather than ground floor level, it would not suffer from excessive overshadowing by the RFH and would have the advantage of direct views across the river. Its elevation above street level would also allow it to become a focus for open air artistic events.

The New Front Door

When it was extended in the early sixties, the orientation of the RFH was directed towards the river. The effect of this was to devalue the status of Belvedere Road; further diminished by the introduction of the raised pedestrian walkway which both visually isolated the South Bank Centre from its immediate urban surroundings and sucked more pedestrian activity away from the street level.

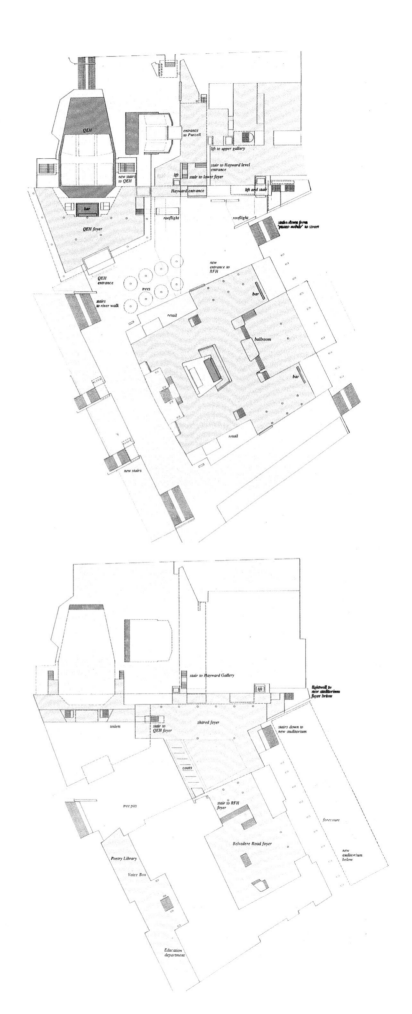

This arrangement should now be reversed and the RFH, and the entire South Bank Centre, reconfigured to address Belvedere Road. This is imperative not only for the Centre – providing it with a clear front door – but also for Belvedere Road itself. Only when the buildings and spaces which line Belvedere Road treat it appropriately will its character as a service road be eliminated, and only then will it be reclaimed for pedestrian use.

Ironically, exactly such an arrangement was proposed subsequent to the

1951 exhibition by Sir Leslie Martin who drew up a scheme for completing the RFH and establishing what he described as the 'principal public entrance' on Belvedere Road. His key idea of a new entrance foyer beneath the Ballroom floor could still be realised.

From this new ground level entrance foyer, stairs and a lift could lead to the existing foyer on level 2, while a direct connection could also be made to the new common foyer underneath the podium.

Locating the New Auditorium

The Belvedere Road frontage to the site has also been selected as the location for the new auditorium. Designed as an underground structure, it would be reached via a single main staircase from the new foyer below the podium. This staircase would be lit by a large vertical rooflight, which would also make its contribution to the spatial definition of the entrance forecourt. The stage has been located at the southern corner of the site, furthest from the alignment of the Northern line tunnels below, and at

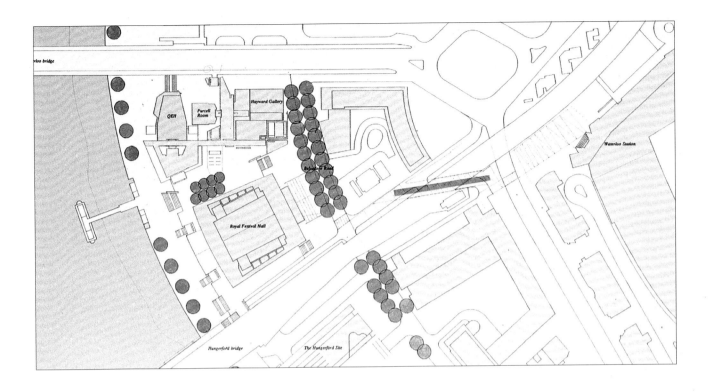

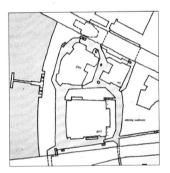 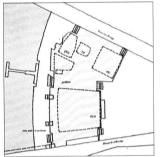 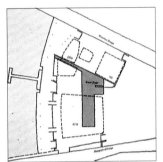 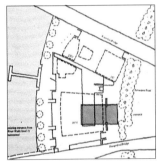

OPPOSITE: Site plan showing pedestrian podium extending the full width of the site, forming a square and linking the three main buildings; FROM ABOVE L TO R: Plan around a single raised external space showing new entrance to Belvedere Road; plans showing existing walkways; new stair to podium; lower foyer; existing entrance from River Walk (level 1) maintained

a position where service connections can be made back to the RFH itself.

There are clear advantages in locating the new auditorium on the one piece of land which remains undeveloped. However, even this approach carries with it a significant premium in terms of specialist engineering. While there is no question as to the desirability of integrating the new auditorium with the existing buildings, the decision to locate it on the core site, as opposed to the Hungerford car-park site, would appropriately be reviewed at a subsequent stage in the master planning process.

The Hayward Redefined

The Hayward Gallery and the QEH were originally planned as separate buildings, linked only by the aesthetic of their construction. The aim now is to link them more directly through the introduction of a new spine, which would provide a route for physical connections and establish a frame for a new entrance to the gallery.

In place of the Hayward's existing foyer, the insertion of a two-storey entrance building is proposed, extending across the site from the podium to Waterloo Bridge. At the lower level (level 2) of the new building, substantial additional space would be available for the sale of tickets and for the gallery shop. At the upper level, linked by a new lift and staircase, an additional floor area of similar dimensions would be available for special exhibitions, conferences or private views. From here, further stairs would lead to a separate entrance to the existing upper galleries, thereby allowing the possibility of mounting independently programmed exhibitions. Of the three existing sculpture terraces, one will be retained (overlooking Waterloo Bridge), one will be adapted to form the link to the upper galleries, and one (overlooking Belvedere Road) will be enclosed in glass.

From the lower level of the foyer, direct access is possible to the rear of the Purcell Room and to the foyer of the QEH. The upper level of the entrance foyer will lead to the new Hayward cafe, located on the roof of the QEH foyer. This extraordinary site, with its views across the city, will provide a remarkable setting. Additional stairs also permit it to be approached from the QEH foyer.

Inverting the Queen Elizabeth Hall Foyer
Just as the interiors of the QEH and the Purcell Room will be improved as part of the current plans, so the foyer which serves them also deserves some modification.

This foyer could be turned inside out: the ribbon of encircling service accommodation could be detached from the perimeter of the foyer and replaced with glass. Planned as a separate structure to the main foyer, it can readily be removed: the effect is to transform the relationship of the foyer both to the river and to the RFH.
The displaced service accommodation would be relocated: the bar would be repositioned at the centre of the foyer, and toilets and cloakrooms moved to the level below. New stairs would be required to link levels and these would be introduced as part of a complete reworking of the existing stairs to the auditoria, which would also incorporate improved disabled access.

Public Activities in the Royal Festival Hall
The creation of the new entrance from Belvedere Road, the formation of the new common foyer beneath the podium, and the construction of the

Hayward cafe, will provide an opportunity to reconsider the disposition of a number of public activities within the RFH itself. The details of such a review are not, however, within the scope of the master plan.

Pedestrians
The solution to improving the lot of pedestrians is not to elevate them above the matrix of roads that cross the site, but to return them to street level. The various footbridges that link the site back to Waterloo will therefore be removed; all proposals for the introduction of footbridges have been dis regarded.

Accompanying this change it would be necessary to introduce some environmental improvement to the pedestrian routes. The greatest would result simply from the increase in density of use, and from the sense of inhabitation that this would engender.

As this implies, the adoption of the Lifschutz Davidson proposals for the creation of a new pedestrian square at ground level outside Waterloo Station would be recommended. However, the proposal for an extended footbridge linking Waterloo directly to the river would not be advocated, as it would not reinforce street level activity. Any improvements to the existing Hungerford footbridge would be desirable as would any further visual definition of the ends of the footbridge.

Deliveries and Collections
These proposals generally adopt the servicing strategy set out within the competition brief. The main service entrance to the RFH is maintained and improved adjacent to Hungerford Bridge; the Hayward Gallery delivery dock is relocated to allow direct access from Belvedere Road; goods access to the QEH and the Purcell Room is reorganised to receive vehicles from under Waterloo Bridge.

While these arrangements satisfy current requirements, some consideration should be given to the long term recla-

mation of the Waterloo Bridge site (currently occupied by the National Film Theatre and the Museum of Moving Image) for partial use by the South Bank Centre: if service access to the Hayward Gallery and the South Bank Centre could be provided here, the need for vehicular use of the river walkway could be avoided entirely.

The Wider Context
Belvedere Road has the potential to become a key component of the city's infrastructure, providing a direct connection between Westminster Bridge and Blackfriars Bridge, and hence between the seat of government and the City of London.

In order to reinforce this idea, any strategy for the South Bank should concentrate its resources on improving Belvedere Road itself. Most importantly these improvements should be introduced throughout the length of the road, emphasising its continuity and its value as a route. Secondly, the value of creating stronger connections between Belvedere Road and York Road, and Belvedere Road and Stamford Street are stressed in this proposal. Thirdly, the principle that the buildings and spaces that line Belvedere Road should address the street is encouraged.

Certainly it is this hierarchy of relationships that should define the organisation of any new buildings constructed on the Hungerford car-park site. The merits of placing a building on this site are considerable. More people would be attracted to follow the river walk; more people would use a (redesigned) Jubilee Gardens. The Hungerford Bridge would impose itself less on its surroundings, while any servicing required could be accommodated.

This may still prove to be an appropriate site for the new auditorium. It may also offer an ideal site for a new NFT and Film Museum, a distinctive building overlooking a modern landscape, beneath which all the car parking could be accommodated.

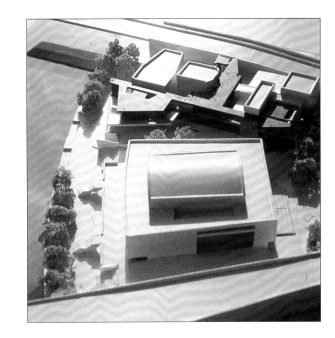

JEREMY DIXON & EDWARD JONES

The South Bank Centre

The South Bank Centre is an enigmatic combination of extraordinary opportunities and irritating practical difficulties. To understand these one has to have a brief look at the history. It is unusual to group cultural buildings together in the manner of the South Bank and it is also unusual that their location is remote from the historic centre of the city. The South Bank complex evolves from the Festival of Britain. The Festival fits with the long history of the South Bank as the place of pleasure gardens, theatre and alternative life. The Thames, as a broad tidal river, has always divided north from south London. Thus the cultural complex belongs to the history of separation from the cities of Westminster and London. Cut off by the road and rail bridge approaches, as well as the river, the site is virtually an island.

The remoteness puts a particular emphasis on the transport systems that link the north to the south. Clearly visible are the bridges crossing the Thames but more important in use are the underground and other train systems. Again, a paradox: the image whereby the South Bank Centre is known is that which is seen across the river from the North Bank but the main direction of arrival is from Waterloo Station; front and back are fundamentally confused. The South Bank Centre sits on the bend in the river surveying the whole history of London from Westminster to the City. It is a strategic site, but how is this potential to be harnessed? The architects came to feel that the combination of history, transport systems and city geography suggests that the South Bank Centre is a special and untypical part of the city characterised by a sense of 'otherness' rather than a place that should be redefined as part of the normal city typology of streets and squares.

The South Bank Centre has grown up as a collage of contemporary urban ideas. The riverside 'city beautiful' becomes 'heroic modernism' in the foyers of the Festival Hall. The ad hoc planning of the Festival of Britain becomes the 'new brutalism' of upper level walkways. The result is quite particular and interesting and should be given respect. It is by no means clear that some buildings are good and some are bad. The architects' proposals for the existing site are thus quite simple:

Consolidate the upper level walkways into a unifying deck, a plinth that brings together all the arts venues and puts the Festival Hall foyer at the centre. Clearly relate this platform to the riverside walk by a bank of steps that bends the upper surface towards the river edge. Adjust the micro-climate, particularly in relation to the prevailing wind, with local sails and other deflectors. Underneath this consolidated plinth create an area for service and support that is not accessible to the public. Rework the main entrance to the Festival Hall including a vehicle drop-off point to give the complex a 'front' on Belvedere Road. Add a new foyer between the Hayward Gallery and Queen Elizabeth Hall that is architecturally distinct from the work of the 50s and 60s.

The logic of the main move, the consolidation of the upper level deck, is supported by the ambiguity of the levels generally around the site. There is not an obvious datum. If we consider the levels, there are pedestrians and traffic at high level on Waterloo Bridge and Hungerford Bridge, together with the concourse of Waterloo Station. There are the existing first level decks, there is the riverside walk, the river beach and the varying level of the tide. None of these are at ordinary ground level. There is an interpretation of the

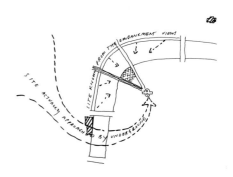

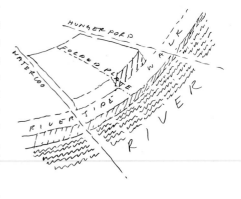

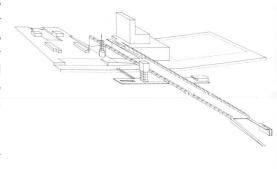

site that focuses on the eccentricity of the levels rather than on the task of normalising around street and ground level.

There is little room on the site for major new architectural gestures. If there is to be an exciting new dimension it will have to come from opportunities outside the core site and particularly in relation to the river.

It is proposed that Hungerford railway bridge should be covered by an abstract rectangular platform. This would become a new place in the city. It would take advantage of the extraordinary view up the Thames past Westminster where bridge follows bridge; the view painted by Monet as he sat in his Savoy bedroom. This would not only be a marvellous place for exhibitions but would link symbolically the North and South Banks. It would also overcome that other conundrum, the resolution of the routes generated from Waterloo Station. Considering the needs of commuters and South Bank visitors there is a case for a pedestrian route on both sides of Hungerford Bridge. The railway line always gets in the way. By providing a unifying destination that is above the railway line the system automatically works. There would have to be escalators and travelators, but these elaborations would be of worth.

In programming the new works the South Bank needs dramatic early successes to gain the public confidence in the project that will lead to successful fund-raising. The project needs to make early moves where relatively small amounts of money have a disproportionate effect. Covering the railway bridge may not solve any of the perceived problems but for five million pounds a dramatic change takes place that strategically harnesses the river as the most important under-used opportunity in the area.

Similarly, the tidal river presents the possibility of accommodation on floating islands. At this lowest level of the

OPPOSITE PAGE, FROM ABOVE: Monet's view of Charing Cross Bridge, the inspiration for the pedestrian terrace; the dilemma of front and back; new plinth as folded plate; Hungerford terrace axonometric, a new place in London

37

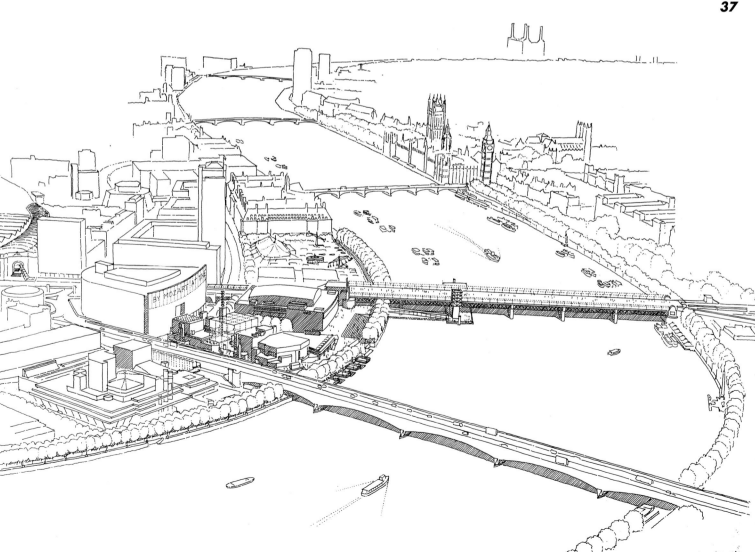

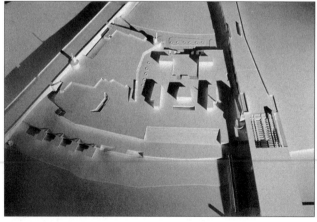 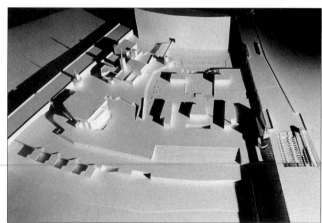

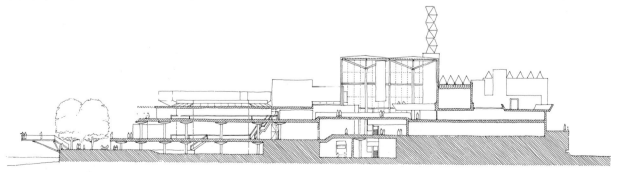

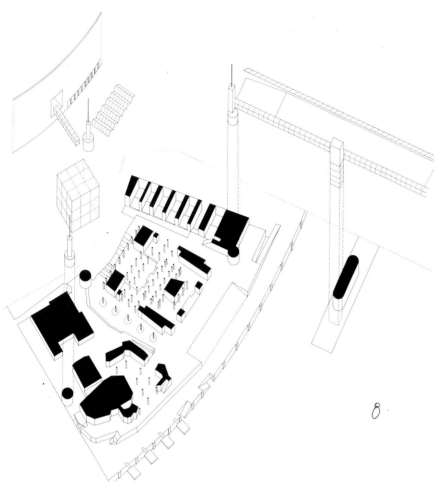

Jeremy Dixon & Edward Jones

39

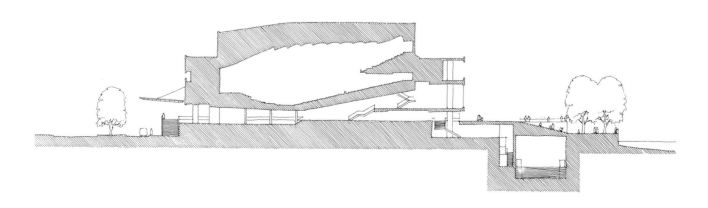

site there are surprising views up and down the river under the bridges. Restaurants and even gallery spaces would become unexpectedly placed with a constantly changing vertical relationship to the new terrace on the bridge. Linking these two categories together would produce special solutions which would themselves become memorable. This might be said to be the role of the master planner – to create inventive challenges for the subsequent designers.

What should the South Bank be like?

What does it mean to relate one art form to another? There is plenty of evidence that architectural determinism does not work in this area. Artists are particularly resistant to being told what to do by buildings. What is needed is an open context that does not prejudge the opportunities that might subsequently be taken. What is needed might be described as a quality of 'benign anarchy.'

Any review of the possibility of creative partnership between the various South Bank activities should include the

National Theatre and film, video and photography as represented by the National Film Institute and MOMI. If there is an area where the arts can spark off one another it is most likely to be in the fringes between the more traditional art forms and those represented by film and photography. The fact that these are omitted from the present brief removes the possibility of speculating about the manifestation of such overlaps. The architects felt very strongly that all the arts institutions on the South Bank should get together to

make the most of the larger potential.

It was felt to be a mistake to make gestural new architectural forms. The excitement should come from what actually happens on the South Bank. For instance the most radical suggestion for the car park and Jubilee Gardens site is to do nothing at all. This area would be left as the major temporary festival site in London. The special nature of the location would demand from the designers of such festivals fantastic visual ideas. What would actually happen on this part of the site would be as a result of liberating the potential rather than making specific architectural proposals.

To what extent should the South Bank be more commercial? There is a version of the success of the South Bank that sees its potential as an arts-orientated shopping centre. The architects were concerned with the general tendency to reduce all public places to shopping centres. If one sees part of the character of the South Bank Centre as its 'otherness' and untypicality, it is perhaps interesting to concentrate on the arts uses and to give them space. The architects interpreted their role as making a few practical suggestions for the existing buildings together with a look beyond the site for the new exciting and dramatic territories that might represent the hidden potential of this extraordinary site. The image of the South Bank should be a constantly changing one reflecting the activities that are inherent within the art forms. If the place works well and there are obvious and well-organised opportunities, the image will look after itself.

SIR NORMAN FOSTER AND PARTNERS

Rebuilding the South Bank brings challenges at many levels. As a cultural centre it has an international reputation for the quality of performances and exhibitions which it hosts. In the average Londoner's perception, however, it is a hostile uninviting area housed in a disparate collection of buildings offering no other attraction than the events they house. To merge these perceptions requires change, not only for the buildings themselves, but for their wider setting. The South Bank is part of a vibrant community, which is slowly transforming the area and generating a whole new vitality. The opportunity exists, through millennium funding, to make the Arts Centre the major catalyst for this change and the symbol of its success. Doubling the attendance

figures will also bring potentially negative pressures such as increased traffic. What is important however is that these potential advantages and disadvantages are recognised and openly discussed prior to and during the change.

The blurring of the edges around the South Bank, its integration into its wider setting will help this process enormously. Today the buildings are seen as an inconvenient barrier by commuters, things to be climbed over; while for the local population the activities housed inside the buildings often seem irrelevant and of no interest. Here opportunities exist to create new spaces not only inside formal structures but through using external areas to create a home for new activities, ones which

will attract people throughout the day and night.

The element which will seize the collective imagination, however, is that of a new structure – the physical reshaping of the performance and exhibition spaces to address current deficiencies and accommodate new demands. Such a structure must build on the best of what exists, be sensitive to its context, open in its approach and striking in its form to act as a symbol for the new millennium.

We are convinced that the opportunity exists to transform the South Bank and to make it a destination for everyone. The opportunity exists and today it is achievable. We must seize it and promote the South Bank to the full to maximise this potential.

42

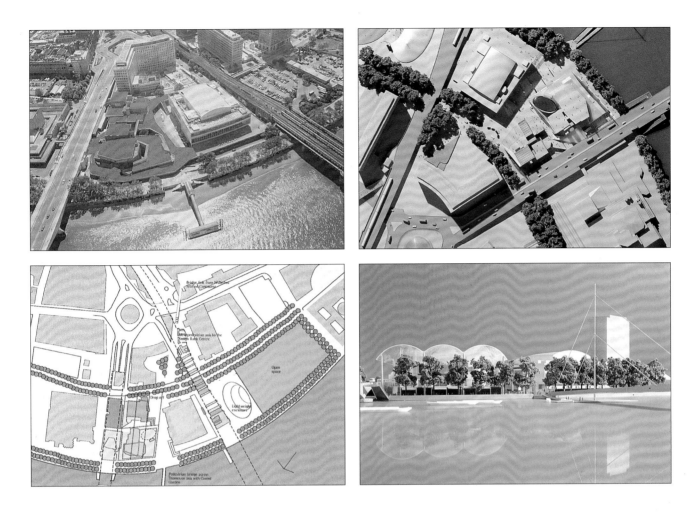

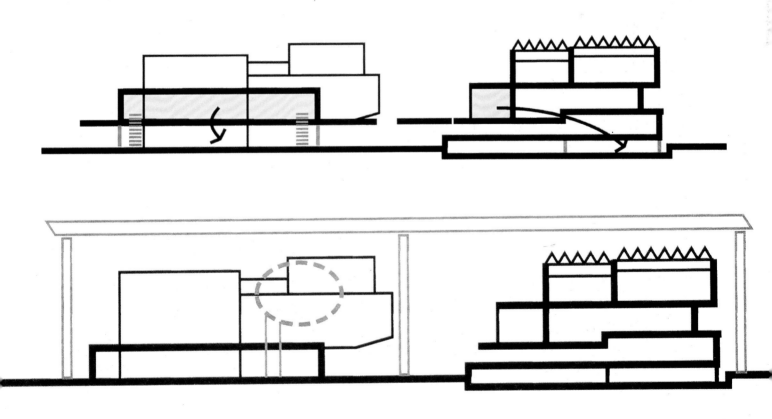

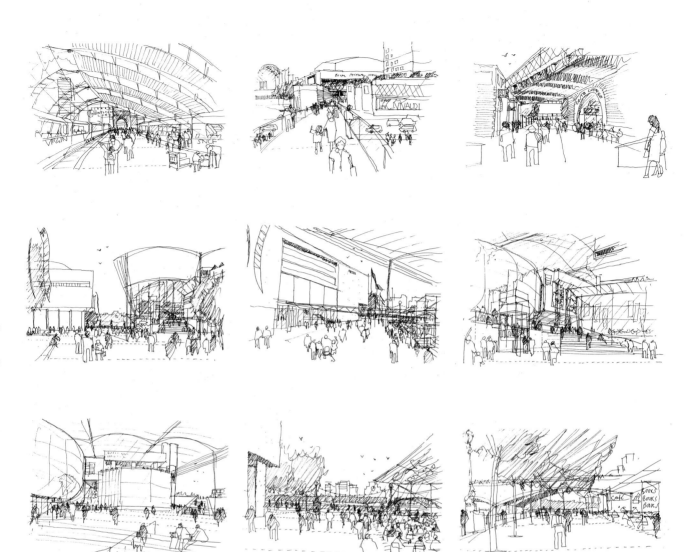

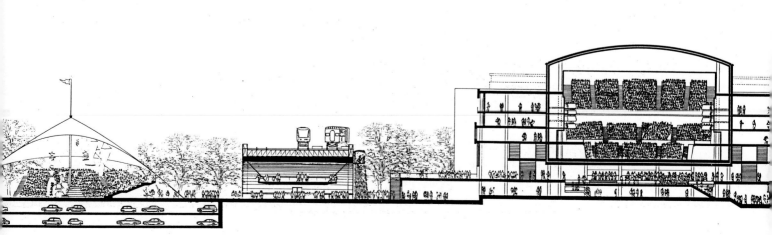

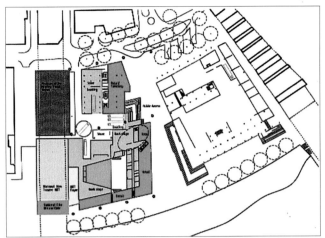

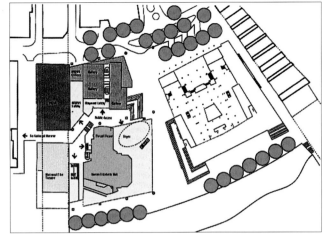

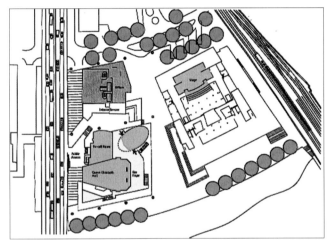

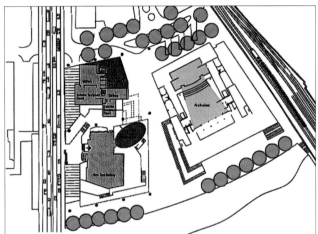

PAGE 43, FROM ABOVE LEFT: Hostile walkways and unusable terraces and roofs dominate site; plan of a framework for the wider area of the South Bank; diagram showing how the QEH foyer and the Hayward Gallery entrance would be moved, temporarily, under the podium of the QEH and car park of the Hayward Gallery; diagram showing the new canopy roof and the shell of a new auditorium constructed; OPPOSITE L TO R: Arriving from Paris at Waterloo; crossing York Road; down to ground level; leading to the new entrance; turning left into the RFH; or right to the new Art Centre; to the first level entrance to the concert hall; back to ground level; and so to the waterfront shops and cafes linked to the NFT; section; FROM ABOVE, L TO R: Plan showing that at ground level, the main entrance links the new Arts Centre to the RFH; plan showing that the first level gives access to all facilities and leads to Waterloo Bridge; plan showing new auditorium of the second level; plan showing the roofs of the QEH, Purcell Room and the new auditorium which are now usable space

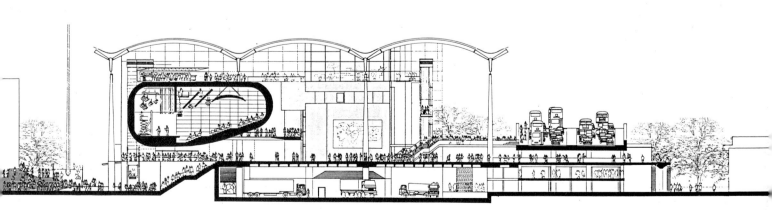

The Role of Cultural Centres in the Twenty-First Century

In considering some well-known examples of cultural centres in Europe, one immediately notices how the main difficulties and problems are not to do with the building itself, but rather with their relationship and connection to the city, whether this is ancient or modern.

This can be seen in the Kulturforum quarter in Berlin, or in the Centre Pompidou in Paris and clearly also in the South Bank Centre. One might add that the structure of cultural centres has become so heterogeneous, stratified and flexible in its layout as to often compete with the very idea of the city. Other issues come to mind in this regard, which have to do with the role a cultural centre will necessarily play in the twenty-first century: the generosity with which almost anything can nowadays be considered culture, the way in which culture is today frequently implying notions of information and amusement, the way in which culture has become a financial enterprise, and the fact that cultural centres have become symbolic urban landmarks.

Now, coming to the specific case of the South Bank Centre in London, we believe one should put in historical perspective the distance which divides us from the buildings forming this Cultural Centre, on one hand; but on the other the proximity which draws us to them. Less than forty years have passed since the South Bank assumed its present shape, and for architecture this is a very short span of time. Because of this, probably all that the buildings need is a special maintenance; instead, what will require a unique effort will be the urban connections: with the South London quarters, with the road network, with the pedestrian realm, with the other facades along the river front, with the railway and underground lines, all in an effort to produce urban density.

The theme of the bunker-like facades of the South Bank, which still heats the souls of many should in our opinion be seen as only part of the problem; certainly it cannot compete with other more structural questions, such as the identity of the place and its functional and symbolic significance as a node of the city.

Lastly, we believe one should take up the opportunity of a possible renewal of the South Bank Centre, to define and draw an overall strategy in

48

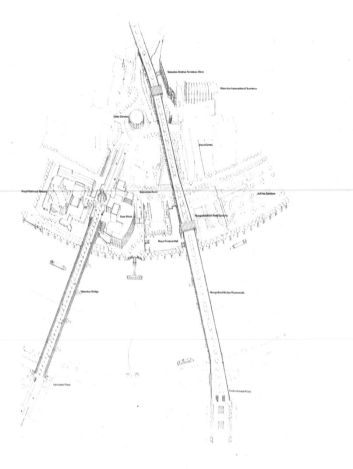

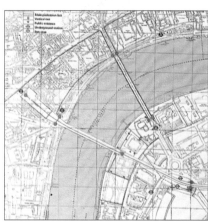

the museums and cultural facilities of London: the science, technique and nature museums in South Kensington, the history and past museums in Trafalgar Square and in Bloomsbury, and the contemporary cultural facilities along the Thames.

Presently the South Bank Cultural Centre is a confused assembly of buildings poorly connected and related to one another, yet with a great potential for interaction. Some problems derive from the original design, some from the modifications over the last twenty-five to forty years; recent problems are related to maintenance and functionality.

Besides, each building fosters a different and conflicting 'architectural composition': the Royal Festival Hall has classical proportions and sharply cut edges, the Hayward Gallery and the Queen Elizabeth Hall celebrate long distance urban connections and the variety of cityscapcs, the National Theatre composes an elegant river scenario based on horizontal strata and vertical towers, and the National Film Institute shyly hides itself under Waterloo Bridge.

This cultural ensemble becomes evident at an urban level way of four emerging points, which can be read from two adjacent tall bridges: the NT cluster of towers, the RFH barrel roof, the Hayward and the QEH. Because

OPPOSITE LEFT: Plan showing landscaping of Waterloo Bridge and building of new panoramic promenade over Hungerford Bridge, improving north and south connections to South Bank Centre; OPPOSITE RIGHT: Maps showing vehicular routes; main pedestrian links; BELOW L TO R: River piazza level plan; Waterloo Bridge level plan; QEH, Hayward Gallery level; axonometric plan of functions; new hall looking towards Waterloo Bridge entrance; OVERLEAF L TO R: Aerial view of three blocks composing the South Bank Cultural Centre; South Bank Centre from Hungerford Bridge; South Bank Centre from Waterloo Bridge canopy; core block from Thames; glazed facade connecting Belvedere road to riverwalk; PAGE 51, FROM ABOVE L TO R: RFH and Hungerford Bridge seen from Hayward Gallery terrace; RFH seen from QEH foyer; Hayward Gallery entrance seen from the hall; NFT, MOMI entrance seen from the hall; new core block and RFH from the north

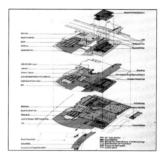

49

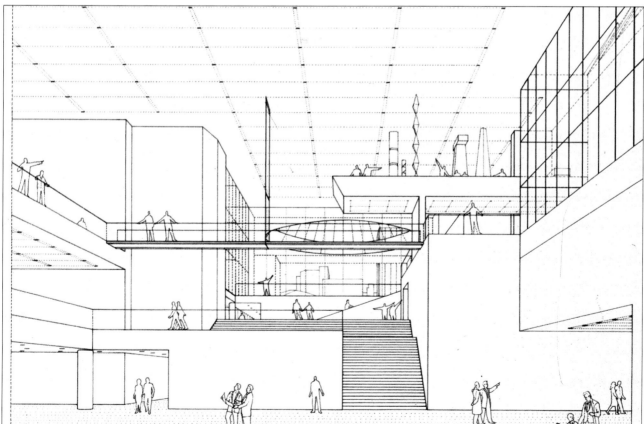

HAYWARD GALLERY

NATIONAL FILM THEATRE
MUSEUM OF THE MOVING IMAGE

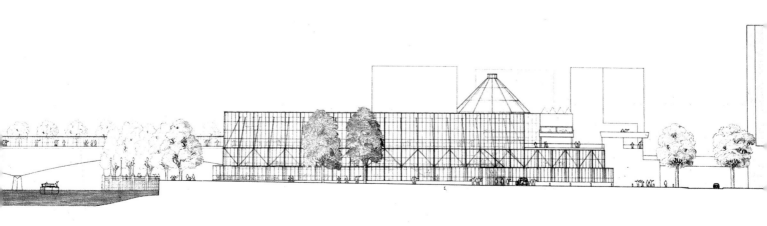

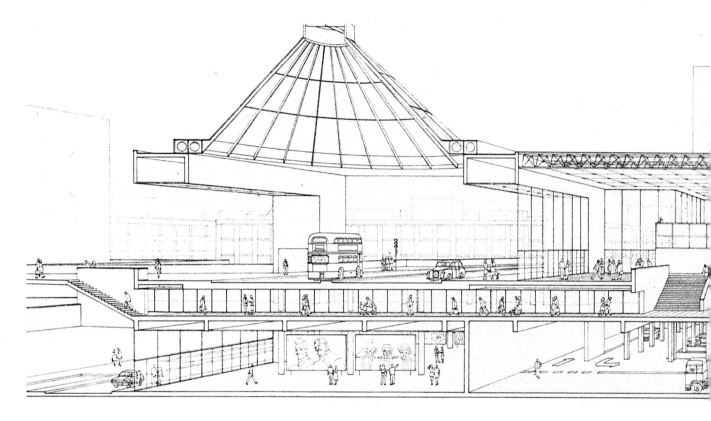

of their heterogeneity, the architects did not insert yet another architectural object; instead, they reduced their number from four to three, by making a single visual block out of the Hayward Gallery and the QEH (Core Block). The South Bank Centre will comprise three clear urban blocks of similar sizes and proportions: the RFH to the south-west, the Core Block in the middle, and the NT to the north-east.

The architects focused the in-between routes of buildings rather than the buildings in themselves. The new project is based on an interrupted interior linear connection stretching from the RFH to the NT, via the new Core Block. These are stops in a linear progression of internal spaces: from the Hungerford Bridge one enters the RFH, crosses the new River Piazza (or, alternatively, one uses the underground passage), and enters the new hall between the HG and the QEH, one crosses Waterloo Bridge (or, alternatively, uses the passage under the bridge), and enters the

NT.

This organisational spine acts as a promenade whence to enter what formerly were different buildings and now are different facilities; it is a simple and easy to understand space, capable of absorbing different situations and uses. As a route, it is directional and always related to ground level; for this reason, it radically opposes the unending complexity of the existing exterior ramps, stairs, walkways and terraces. In the project, these are partly demolished and partly retained in the new interior space.

As in plan, also in section, the hall exploits of existing conditions; these are inflected to suit new circulation patterns and functional requirements. The levels of the new hall relate to existing levels: the Hayward Gallery and of the NFI, the QEH, the New Auditorium, the new River Piazza and Waterloo Bridge.

The new hall becomes the interior landmark space not only of the core

block, but of the entire South Bank Centre; it will be enlivened by shops, cafes, performances, exhibitions and amusements of all kinds. People will first arrive here, then will decide what to do.

The core block will be organised more simply than it is now; each institution within (NFT, Hayward Gallery, QEH, Purçell Room) will exchange some of its present autonomy for greater integration. This will involve a novel management concept: unity rather than fragmentation, support rather than competition.

The ground level of the core block will contain the reserved parking and the delivery docks serving the different institutions within; this will be accessed from the Belvedere Road and will connect to the floors above by way of new lifts. The principal public restaurant/cafe will also be at ground level, overlooking the river.

The required local extensions and improvements of the single institutions will

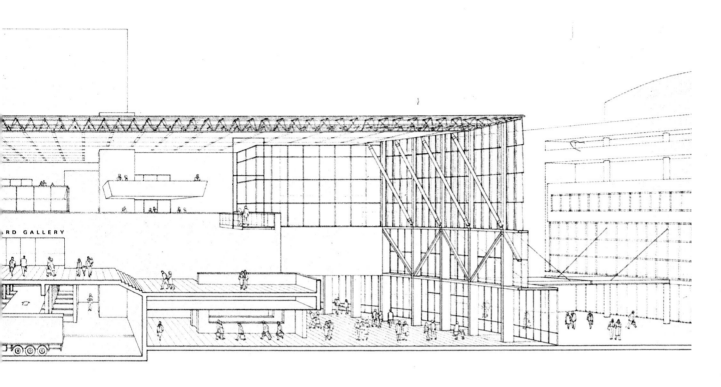

happen in the context of the unified block, extending the building upward or occupying previously exterior walkways or terraces. The Hayward Gallery gains new exhibition rooms on the top and reorganises its entry sequence; the QEH gains a new auditorium above the Purcell Room and a new lobby facing the new hall.

The future success of the South Bank Centre will depend on the simplicity and quality of the urban connections rather than on their quantity. At present, in the wider area, the ineffectiveness of many connections appears related to their dislocation, quality and quantity. So, Gregotti's project selects new principal entrances to the South Bank Centre grounds: from Waterloo Bridge, from Hungerford Bridge and from Waterloo Station. They intend to normalise the urban relationships between the South Bank Centre and the surrounding urban context.

To achieve this, the system of walkways within the South Bank Centre is demolished and connecting the South Bank Centre is linked to the Waterloo Station and the ground level continuity is reinforced at level 0.00, while realistically accepting the presence of the traffic bridges/viaducts as boundary elements of the site. Our scheme in fact proposes to reinforce the visual presence of the bridges, to fit the grand horizontal scale of the Thames; both the Hungerford Bridge and Waterloo Bridge become virtually inhabited elements.

Waterloo Bridge loses its principally utilitarian overtone and becomes an urban gateway to the South Bank Cenre; two side pergolas and a tree line down the middle.

Hungerford Bridge/viaduct becomes an important uninterrupted pedestrian connection from Charing to Waterloo East, via the South Bank Centre and station. A grand panoramic promenade, sitting above the existing structural trusses and entered directly from the ticket hall of Charing Cross Station, will replace tortuous passage and way-through to the Strand. It should be emphasised that the renovation and upgrading of the two river bridges should be considered separate from the core site part of the project: they can be disjointed, and built at a later date. The two principal wyas of access to the South Bank Centre from Waterloo Station (both domestic and international) are the Hungerford Bridge/Viaduct pedestrian promenade (easily accessible upon exiting the Station), and the diagonal passage under the Hungerford Viaduct, connecting the piazza along the Belvedere Road behind the RFH.

The Hungerford car park site is confirmed as the prime parking basin for the area. Planned on two split levels and profiled to look contiguous with the adjacent Jubilee Gardens, it is confirmed as part of the leisure walk along the Thames.

Perspective longitudinal section of hall

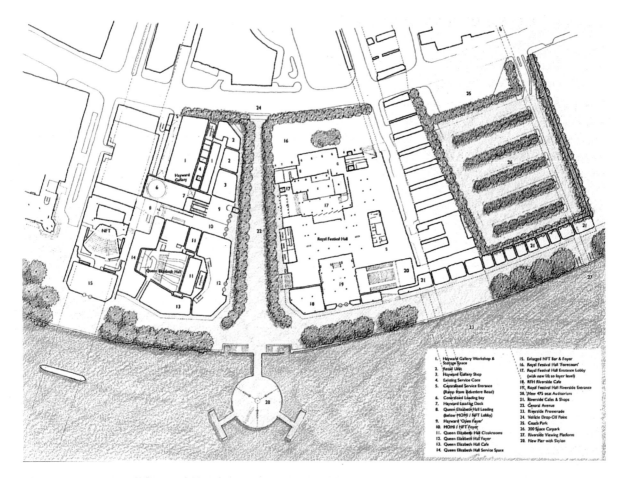

1. Hayward Gallery Workshop & Storage Space
2. Retail Units
3. Hayward Gallery Shop
4. Existing Service Core
5. Centralised Service Entrance (Ramp from Belvedere Road)
6. Centralised Loading bay
7. Hayward Loading Dock
8. Queen Elizabeth Hall Loading (below MOMI / NFT Lobby)
9. Hayward 'Open Foyer'
10. MOMI / NFT Foyer
11. Queen Elizabeth Hall Cloakrooms
12. Queen Elizabeth Hall Foyer
13. Queen Elizabeth Hall Cafe
14. Queen Elizabeth Hall Service Space
15. Enlarged NFT Bar & Foyer
16. Royal Festival Hall 'Forecourt'
17. Royal Festival Hall Entrance Lobby (with new lift to foyer level)
18. RFH Riverside Cafe
19. Royal Festival Hall Riverside Entrance
20. New 475 seat Auditorium
21. Riverside Cafes & Shops
22. Central Avenue
23. Riverside Promenade
24. Vehicle Drop-Off Point
25. Coach Park
26. 300 Space Carpark
27. Riverside Viewing Platform
28. New Pier with Skylon

54

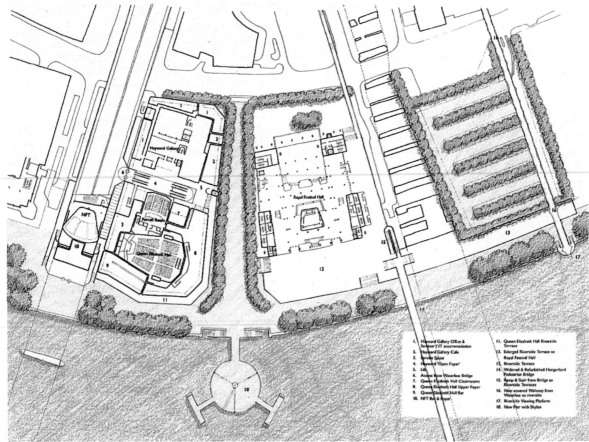

1. Hayward Gallery Office & Seminar / IT accommodation
2. Hayward Gallery Cafe
3. Service Space
4. Hayward 'Open Foyer'
5. Lifts
6. Access from Waterloo Bridge
7. Queen Elizabeth Hall Cloakrooms
8. Queen Elizabeth Hall Upper Foyer
9. Queen Elizabeth Hall Bar
10. NFT Bar & Foyer
11. Queen Elizabeth Hall Riverside Terrace
12. Enlarged Riverside Terrace to Royal Festival Hall
13. Riverside Terrace
14. Widened & Refurbished Hungerford Pedestrian Bridge
15. Ramp & Stair from Bridge to Riverside Terraces
16. New covered Walkway from Waterloo to riverside
17. Riverside Viewing Platform
18. New Pier with Skylon

MICHAEL HOPKINS AND PARTNERS

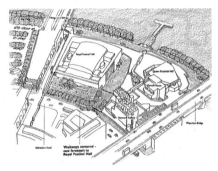

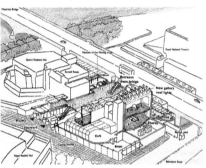

The Role of the South Bank as a Cultural Centre

First thoughts: 'I like the South Bank. My first childhood visit to London was with my father in 1951. Upon the train from Dorset to Waterloo – then wham! straight into the Festival. It was modern, quite unlike anything that I had experienced. I remember the Dome of Discovery, the Skylon and eating outside on white metal chairs with funny splayed legs.

The Festival Hall is not part of that first mind picture – that came later. The strongest image was the great river panorama with its bend and what must be *London* on the far side. I would like to think that the visit started me off as an architect, but I can't make that direct connection.

I still get that sense of anticipation and excitement when I visit the South Bank today. Particularly on foot and at night when the scruffy bits recede. The juxtaposition of the great, bright, welcoming interior of the Festival Hall with the dark river and the twinkling lights of the River Walk and beyond the far bank, magic! It is always going to be a place that you visit rather than pass through. The river and the rail tracks will always mean that the South Bank is separated from adjoining districts. However, at the city scale and in a city of wide cultural activity, it is not remote in any sense. London is made up of an open network of distinct districts. Places that have an individual character and identity and which flourish without having an immediate hinterland of residential population to draw upon for support.'

The Wider Context

Any master plan for 'between the bridges' of the South Bank Centre must look at the wider neighbourhood to set the context.

Downstream, the National Theatre is already preparing its own plan, which at present proposes the demolition of the walkways and a reorganisation of traffic and entrances at ground level. Upstream, the car park site must soon be under active consideration for a major new Arts

55

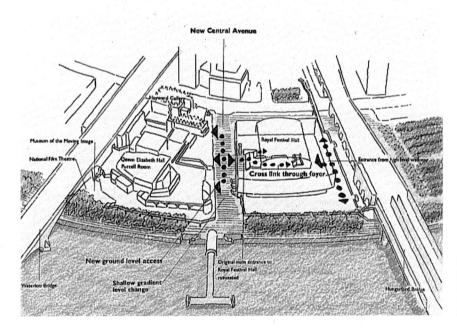

OPPOSITE, FROM ABOVE: Ground-floor plan; first-floor plan; FROM ABOVE: Plan showing the new forecourt for the Royal Festival Hall; plan of Hayward Gallery and MOMI; plan showing the new central avenue

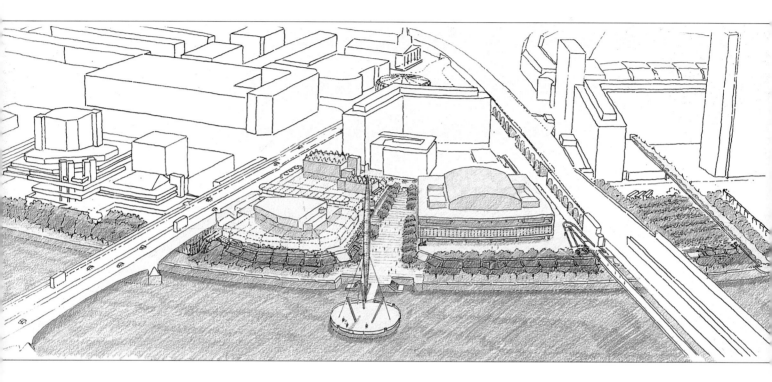

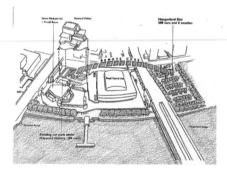
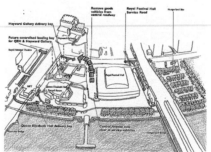
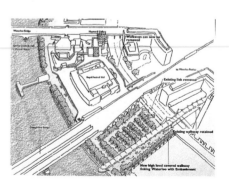

FROM ABOVE L TO R: Aerial view; plan showing the removal of cars from the core area; plan showing the removal of goods vehicles to the perimeter; plan showing the construction of a covered link between Waterloo and the River

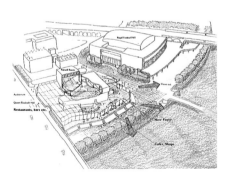
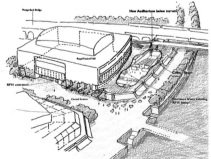
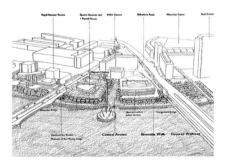

FROM ABOVE L TO R: View of the Central
Avenue and Riverside Walk; plan of the QEH
and the Purcell Room; plan of the RFH
improvements and new auditorium; plan of
the final results

building – with parking relegated below ground.

Upstream again, Jubilee Gardens will be an excavation and works site for the Jubilee Line until nearly the end of the century. Thought should be given to what opportunities this site will offer in the future. Further upstream, but still within the orbit of the South Bank Centre, there is County Hall. Although lost as a public London asset, it is set to become a hotel and influence must be brought to bear that it contributes positively to the public realm.

There is also the local business district, a large daytime community, with the Shell Centre, IBM and LWT, all of which help to strengthen the local community and provide a background of everyday city life.

To the south, the Waterloo Terminal will open shortly, offering the potential for the South Bank to welcome to London tens of thousands of tourists each year. To the north, there is the elusive prize of a new or improved pedestrian bridge with travelators across the river, which would unlock the direct link to the West End. Any master plan for the South Bank must account for this possibility, but not be dependent on it.

Having looked wider, it is essential to focus upon the task in hand which is a plan for the South Bank Centre itself.

The South Bank Centre

The South Bank, with its prominent river frontage, has a great sense of place and identity and a rich nucleus of cultural activities. At present, with six million visitors a year, similar in number to the British Museum or the whole of the South Kensington museum complex, there is a strong customer base on which to build. Taking all the centres of cultural activity in London it is the one with the space and opportunity to extend the range of facilities and activities on offer.

The open foyer policy of the Festival Hall has done much to encourage all age groups to say 'Let's go to the South Bank' in the same way as the young

plan to go to Covent Garden, to promenade, to browse or be entertained. The demand for cultural events that are also fun will increase. As we move into the 21st century, the technology of information will make the experience of art, literature, music and drama available at home at the touch of a button. As a result, far from making public places for the arts redundant, I believe that appetites will be whetted at home and stimulated to see, hear and feel the real thing. Particularly they will seek the sense of occasion, the treat, the outing, the congregation with others and the visit to a special place. The South Bank Centre, together with the National Theatre and the Film Thea-tre, representing all the arts at an international level, in their special river setting with space for cafes and restaurants and room to promenade under trees with a great view, provides that special place.

Circulation for visitors and services is awkward and confused. Entrances are obscure, the Queen Elizabeth Hall and the Hayward lack support space and the spaces between the buildings miss the opportunity of providing a public front with interest and activity.

However in any redesign or expansion of the facilities the challenge will be to understand the objectives of the original designers to retain the investment both culturally and financially in the auditoria, foyers and galleries and to reinterpret the architecture without destroying the evidence of public endeavour in the 60s.

At Lord's, more recently at Glyndebourne and now at the House of Commons the architects have been successful at turning plans into built projects. They consult widely, make proposals, demonstrate that it can be done without closing down the institution and, most importantly, they gather the wide support necessary to raise money and obtain approvals.

If appointed at the South Bank, the architects would prepare a master plan, the way to achieve it, then generate support and enthusiasm to get it done.

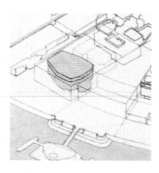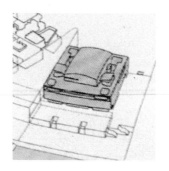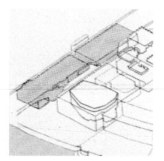

LIFSCHUTZ DAVIDSON

The Core Site

The architects' vision is for the site to acquire a memorable and distinctive architectural quality associated with culture, with pleasure, excitement and spontaneity. Standing at the heart of the site will be a new forum, visible from the city all around and in particular from the north bank of the river, a landmark for the arts. On fine days there will be people milling around its grand portico taking in the view and enjoying impromptu performances. On dark winter evenings crowds will gather inside where, visible through the vast windows of the illuminated space, they will be a magnet for others.

This crystalline space will give people access to the arts within the complex. It will open up the river to the hinterland and connect buildings which stand today separated rather than linked by the spaces between them. It will be the gathering place for the core site and the South Bank as a whole and is the organising principle around which the plan is structured to restore a sense of place and a focus to the site.

The Wider Site

The South Bank is a special but frustrating place. It lies only a mile from the centre of the city on a spectacular loop of the Thames. There are superb transportation links, fine parks and unrivalled facilities for the arts. But the architecture is hostile, the vast buildings which dominate are made of brutal materials and turn their backs on the city to contain all life within. There is also huge waste, of land between the buildings and also of the scarce resources inside them, used for only a few hours during the working day.

So it is proposed that weakness is turned to strength. In partnership with neighbours, and for mutual profit, vacant sites will be colonised, trees and gardens planted, car parks and other facilities shared, pavilions, bandstands and restaurants erected. The new buildings will be small in scale but popular, designed to project colour and life onto the streets. They will contain the latest technology, computers and multi-media and they will be filled with music and art, food and fashion. There will be ferries, pleasure boats and fireworks on the river. Discussions with local landowners show that the need for these projects already exists, indeed some are on the drawing board. This master plan gives them expression.

Inspired by the Festival of Britain, it is proposed that the wider site be developed further as the festival site of London. The model for this vision of an urban festival district already exists in the Tivoli Gardens in Copenhagen and there are other places such as Stockholm, Montreal, Cannes and Edinburgh

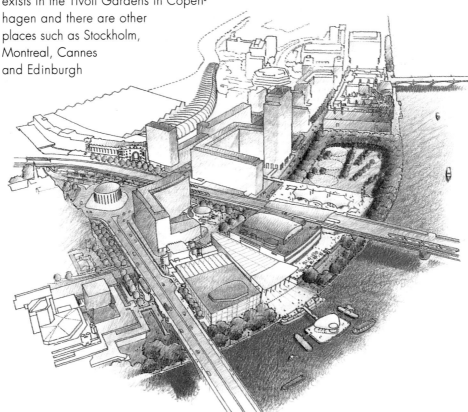

A LANDMARK TO THE ARTS

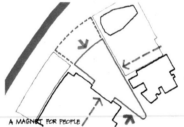

A MAGNET FOR PEOPLE

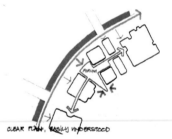

CLEAR PLAN, EASILY UNDERSTOOD

from which we can learn. Just as it was in 1951, festival will be the key to unlocking the potential of the South Bank to give new generations of people an introductions into the arts and the pleasures of architecture, music, painting, film and theatre. In return the South Bank will benefit from new, younger visitors, from grants and private investment flowing into the area and from new buildings and infrastructure. It will lose its municipal, unfriendly image and once again will become a 'tonic to the nation'.

Access

The South Bank probably has the best transport facilities in London and the busiest conjunction of routes. Charing Cross, Waterloo Station, Waterloo East, the International Terminal, several underground stations, major roads and bus routes, river boats, four bridges and a host of other facilities are located there and yet the paradox is that people find it hard to get to the site. The general view is that it is too remote.

The truth is that there may be too

many forms of transport to the South Bank and too little consideration for the pedestrian who has to use them. There has been no understanding that, in the end, people must get out of their cars, trains, coaches, buses and boats to reach the final destination on foot. For wheelchair users, the environment presents appalling challenges and hazards.

Walkways were supposed to free the pedestrian. The unfortunate legacy of the idea of streets in the air was to

A SHELTERED LINK

FLEXIBLE AND EASILY SERVICED

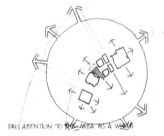

PAY ATTENTION TO THE AREA AS A WHOLE

hand over dominance of the ground to vehicles. Meanwhile, the walkways have not worked. They are confusing, inaccessible and exposed. Yet, amazingly, more overhead walkways are planned to cope with new gyratory roads serving the International Terminal at Waterloo.

The architects plan to demolish most of the walkways and reclaim the ground to give priority to people. They have already made proposals for a new piazza outside Waterloo Station

and a handsome ground level route to the RFH. Proposals for improved pedestrian routes from the south and east of the site and passing under Waterloo Bridge are also supported.

The challenge of finding pleasurable ways for the pedestrian to cross the river from the north bank has never been properly addressed. The architects have previously suggested the replacement of the battered and noisy Hungerford pedestrian route with a wider, sheltered bridge to provide a

spectacular promenade across the Thames.

It is also proposed that visitors to London be offered a route from Covent Garden which leads straight down the hill to Cleopatra's Needle and across to the Core Site by ferry boat. The architects also suggest enhancements to Waterloo Bridge which must be given the same level of attention as the bridges further south, celebrated by light and leading for the first time to an exciting destination on the South Bank.

Master Plan for the South Bank Centre

The South Bank has unrivalled assets: a glorious setting on the river with some of the best views in London; the Royal Festival Hall, a rare example of a well liked twentieth-century building; a location close to the West End and to Waterloo with its new Channel Tunnel Terminal. Most important is the less tangible asset of a dynamic arts and programming policy which attracts a diverse, popular audience and puts the South Bank amongst the most important cultural centres in the world.

The site also presents serious problems – its paradoxical separation from the centre of London, its hostile microclimate and daunting hinterland.

The challenge of formulating a master plan is to propose an idea which is ambitious enough to capture the public imagination, but which also carries conviction as a practical strategy; a grand gesture which must be achieved through a series of controlled interventions. This master plan addresses three major issues arising from the problems and the opportunities of the site: access; image and environment and places and events.

Access

There are three categories of visitor to the South Bank: those who come for a particular purpose, such as attending a ticketed event; those who come to enjoy the atmosphere and those who are passing through, for the most part tourists and commuters. By enabling people to travel through the site easily, and by making their journey an enjoyable experience, the South Bank is made more lively and is able to tempt the third category of visitors to sample its attractions. Improving links across the river will enable the South Bank to take advantage of its proximity to the West End and other centres for the Arts and entertainment in London – Trafalgar Square, Covent Garden, St James' Park and Parliament Square.

The pedestrian walkway on Hungerford Bridge should be rebuilt with travelators and walkways on both sides, to take advantage of the spectacular views up and down the Thames. The travelators would deposit people on the river front promenade; so commuters would pass through, rather than go past, the site on their way to and from Waterloo.

Two new access points are proposed from Waterloo Bridge: a terrace at bridge level in front of the Queen Elizabeth Hall, giving access to the

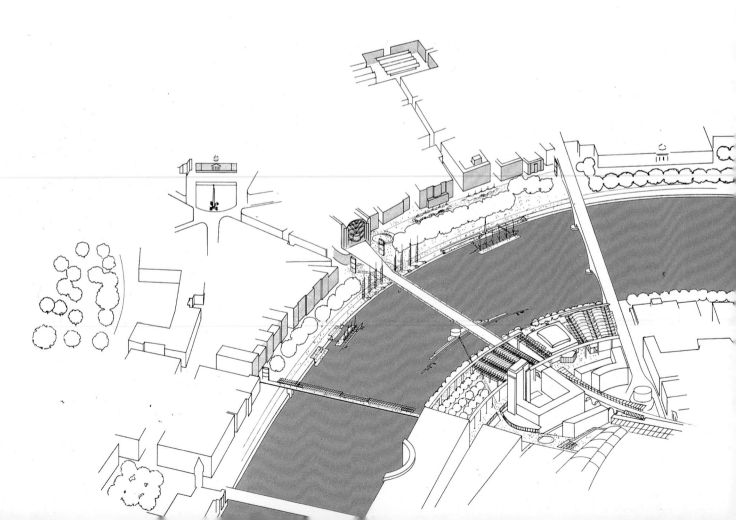

riverside promenade, and a new foyer to MOMI with entrances from the bridge and from ground level.

It is proposed that a new footbridge be constructed from the west side of Jubilee Gardens to the North Bank. It would connect with the promenade level of the South Bank site and with the raised terraces giving access to the main entrance of Waterloo International Terminal.

Constructing an island in the river would reduce the perceived distance of the South Bank Centre from the North Bank. The island would be closer to the South Bank, so that it is seen to be a part of the Centre.

Proposals to form a pedestrian square outside Victory Arch at Waterloo are endorsed, and the suggestion here is to extend the square under the arches of the railway viaduct to give access to a pedestrian link with travelators which would be routed alongside the viaduct, rising over York Road, passing the Shell Centre downstream, and depositing people at a new threshold to the South Bank on the inland side of the RFH.

In conjunction with this, the section of Belvedere Road along the Hungerford car-park site, and up to Waterloo Bridge, would be pedestrianised (with restricted access for service vehicles), re-surfaced and upgraded to form a new public space.

Commuters on their way to the North Bank would be attracted into the site by the convenience of the travelator link and the new accessibility at ground level.

A direct link could be formed from the new Waterloo International entrance, passing over York Road to Jubilee Gardens, giving access to the South Bank and, through the gardens, to the new footbridge crossing the river. The route through the gardens would also create a link with the hotel and recreational development of County Hall.

Image and Environment

There is a general consensus that the approaches to the South Bank are

OPPOSITE: The site in context; FROM ABOVE: View from the north bank at night; aerial view looking southeast; view from Waterloo Bridge; route to Waterloo Station and route to Waterloo International; OVERLEAF: Aerial view from the south with plans of the relationship of different cultural activities, showing circulation at promenade and at ground level

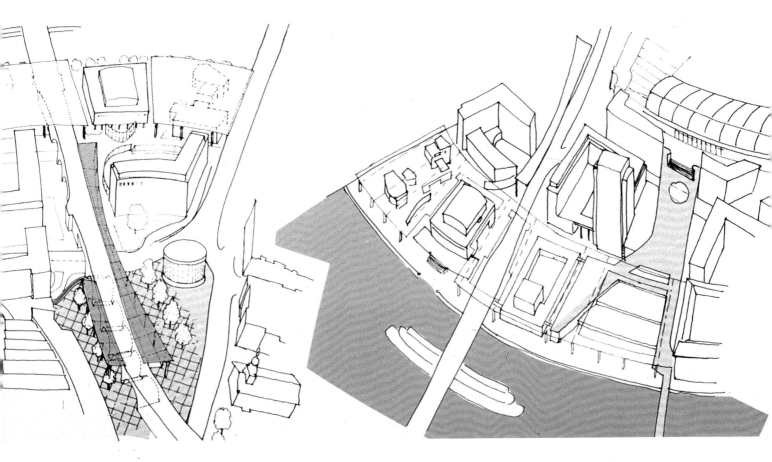

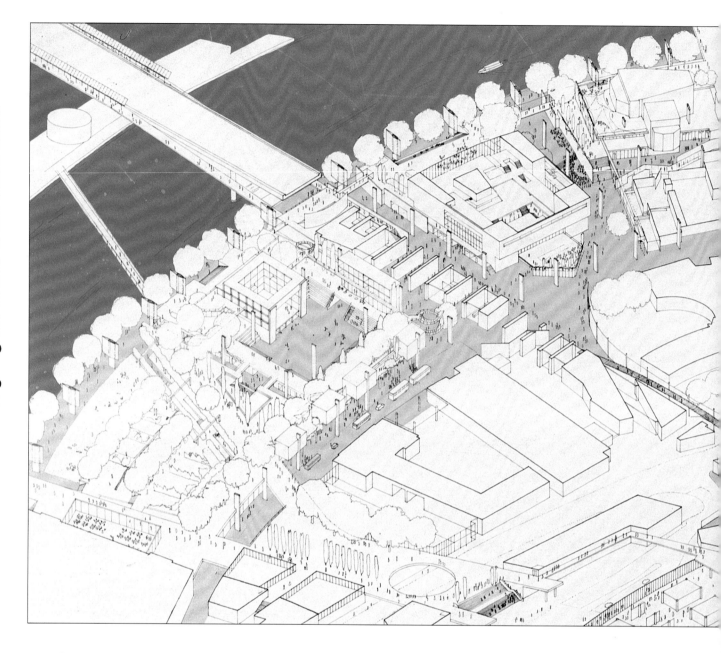

tortuous and uncomfortable and that the character of the site, before reaching the foyers of the buildings, is unattractive and confusing. From the north Bank, the Centre seems remote and is split in half by Hungerford Bridge. From the south it is obscured by a hideous hinterland of traffic, railway arches and ungainly buildings.

This lack of coherence prevents the South Bank from appearing as a single united cultural centre with complementary arts activities. A fundamental intention of the master plan is to create a powerful and unifying idea for the whole site which overcomes its functional and visual fragmentation – a grand gesture for the millennium.

The proposal is to define the area of the South Bank from Waterloo Bridge to County Hall with a roof whose scale is commensurate with the existing buildings on the site and with the expanse of the River Thames, and dominant enough to subsume Hungerford Bridge.

A grid of columns supporting a glass and fabric roof would encompass the whole site, forming a great plane of translucency with the quality of both water and sky. This roof is inclusive and sheltering – a powerful symbol of openness and accessibility. It sails over the existing buildings – the Hayward Gallery, the QEH and the Purcell Room and the new buildings proposed for the Hungerford car-park site. The planes of the roof and the supporting columns frame, but do not touch, the RFH, which remains the architectural set piece of the site. The scale and reflection of this structure will be sufficient to claim the river as the South Bank's aqueous forecourt, lit with floodlights, projection and lasers at night.

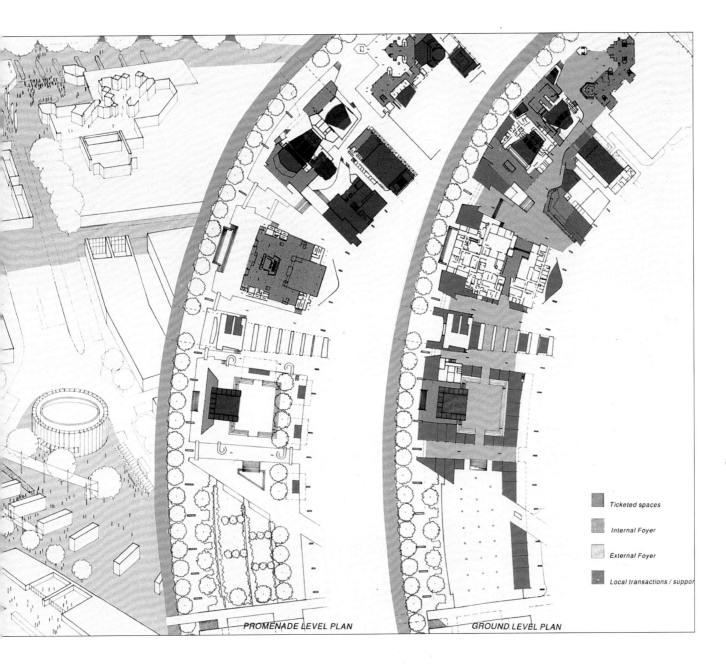

PROMENADE LEVEL PLAN   GROUND LEVEL PLAN

Ticketed spaces

Internal Foyer

External Foyer

Local transactions / support

At the river front, the columns are encased in 'fins' of glass. Seen obliquely from the river walk, the effect of layers of clear glass builds to a watery green colour. At night, coloured light and images will be projected onto the fins, seen reflected in the river from the North Bank. The roof allows the residual spaces between the existing buildings to become places in their own right. The whole site is transformed into a series of 'foyers' which will extend the activities which currently take place in the RFH foyers, creating a great 'market place' for the arts.

Places and Events

The master plan aims to improve access and orientation within the site itself. Pedestrian movement along the embankment with its river views remains vital, but is strongly tied back into the site and connects to Belvedere Road by a series of radial spaces and routes. These routes open up frequent perspectives through the site and across the river.

It is planned to regenerate Belvedere Road by re-structuring vehicle access and lining the edge of the site with buildings which front onto the road. In this way, the South Bank recognises that it is part of Lambeth, and the community to the south of the site. Shops and workshops would be built on Belvedere Road at the Hungerford car park site, with studios, galleries, workshops and other facilities above.

A crucial tactic in this master planning strategy is to create a new route through the centre of the site which links the foyers of the principal buildings and opens out into the square by the NT at its northern end. The route passes under Waterloo Bridge between the British Film Institute and MOMI, runs

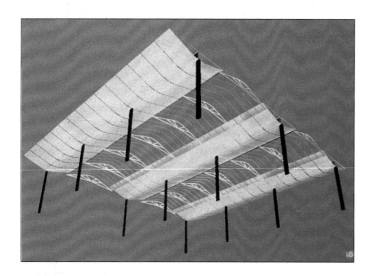
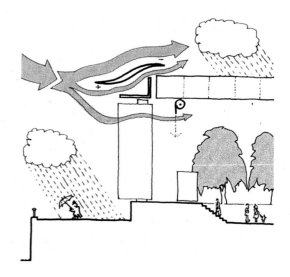

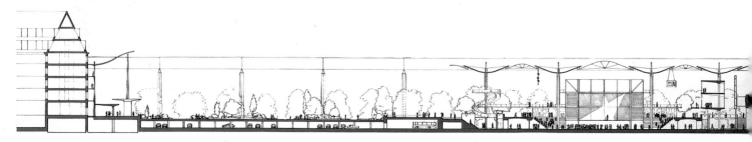

through the Centre of the RFH and then through the railway arches of Hungerford Bridge into a new, major covered public square or forum, which gives access to a new auditorium on the river side.

To form the route, the services area of the RFH is repositioned below a new terrace on the river side of the building and a new entrance is created at ground level facing the arches below Hungerford Bridge.

The route under Waterloo Bridge is formed by demolishing one of the BFI's auditoria (to be replaced at the riverside end of their site). Work to the BFI and MOMI would include providing more prominent front doors onto this route.

A public space is formed between the Hayward Gallery, the QEH, the Purcell Room and the RFH. The foyers of these buildings open onto the space, and cafes and bars would be incorporated into the surrounding buildings and below the riverside terrace.

The success of the exemplary 'open foyers' policy at the RFH suggests a design and management strategy for the whole site. This is to recognise distinctions between different kinds of cultural events – those which are ticketed and take place in an exclusive environment, such as the concert hall or art gallery, and those which are encountered spontaneously and which take place in a freely accessible environment, like the RFH foyers. The foyers provide a theatrical setting for the major events and the intention is to extend such a setting throughout the site.

This would create a milieu shared by concert-goers, exhibition-goers and those who come for recreation, for a drink, to meet friends, to browse in a book shop or watch a platform performance. With this synergetic pattern, the South Bank would combine its cultural cutting edge with the role of cultural pleasure garden.

Such a place could appeal to all sectors of the community,

embrace wide cultural interests and be a forum for London's citizens to debate political and cultural issues. A common ground would be provided for Londoners and visitors alike to gather, to see and be seen, to be part of the city's culture; counteracting the isolating effects of television, video and recorded music.

The South Bank must make the most of the fact that it is 'live', that each performance is unique, that the audience plays its part and is essential to the event. The objective is to create places which will accommodate as wide a variety of performances and events as possible; amplifying the creative potential of the present programming policy. By roofing the site a variety of potential foyer/performance spaces are created, all protected from rain, with the potential for some areas (such as the forum), to become winter gardens protected from the wind by movable, transparent screens.

The spaces created by the master-

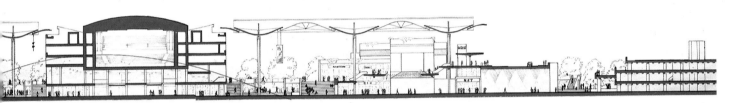

plan are not prescriptive but are intended to support every kind of cultural or communal activity. Some activities would involve movement through the site – processions, carnivals, fashion shows, promenading. Some might involve temporary transformations of space with enclosures, tents or flooding for a water festival or forming an ice rink in the forum. Others would involve performance and public interaction, opera, dance, theatre, circus, comedy, music, films, light shows, video art and debate. Yet more would involve installations – college art shows, sculpture shows, book fairs, art markets, festivals, exhibitions – a London Biennale?

This range of activity would not detract from the more conventional auditoria and gallery programmes, but would be a means to introduce a larger audience to them. Performances in the RFH and QEH could be projected on screens in other parts of the site.

The success of the centre will depend on management and financial resources to sustain the liveliness of the venue. The events taking place will also need the support of amenities which will inhabit the edges of the public spaces. These support facilities would include cafes, bars, interactive video and sound track kiosks, interactive information points, ticket agencies and shops.

The up-river part of the site could also provide offices for agencies working with the homeless. Their location at the South Bank will give the cause of homelessness the weight that it warrants.

The Future

The forces which determine the modern city – geographical dispersal, suburbia, the motor car, privatisation of public space, television, information technology, virtual reality, financial and social inequality and the collapse of social and kinship structures – tend to disperse people into increasing isolation.

Accessible arts centres offer a physical, social and metaphorical meeting place, an open house, to reclaim the idea of society itself and to find in the arts the delightful possibility of sharing new experiences and values.

The regeneration of the South Bank will be seen as catalysing the revival of London itself – a long overdue resurgence of public aspiration and belief in the effectiveness of collective action.

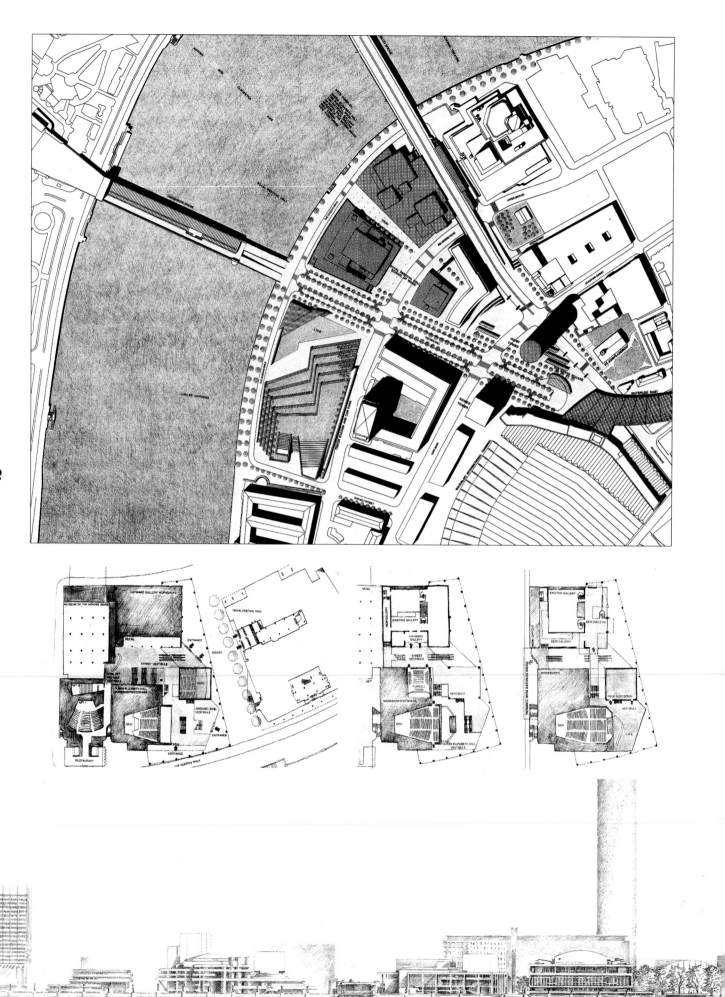

The South Bank Centre – Recovering the True City

Cultural centres were established around the heart of several cities in the fifties with the clear political intention of regenerating the city centre. The Lincoln Center in New York, the Kulturforum in Berlin, the South Bank in London all belong to this mid-century concept of cultural acropolis.

There is little doubt that they did create new cultural centres, but the desired domino effect on revitalising the surrounding districts was only a limited success. This was probably due to the over close adherence to the concept of the functional city where every function is allocated its specific space, so that in reality these cultural centres were, like the Greek Acropolis, pedestals for cultural events 'safely' separated from the toil of a busy city.

Without swinging to an opposite extreme, it is now necessary to consider these cultural centres under the more modern approach to urban design of critical reconstruction; that is, the necessity to respond to all the composing elements that contribute to the complexity and contradictions of urban life through the clear definition of the form and structure of the public space.

However difficult it may be, the single segregated use of part of the city should be avoided to allow the accidental nature of urban encounters to take place. In other words, the mixed-use of the High Street should be allowed to filter across these cultural acropolises to ensure a varied urban activity at any time of the day or night. In this way, the cultural centres will reintegrate into the pattern of public spaces and be accessible to people going through it and not just going to them.

The South Bank is an important part of London's architectural heritage of the fifties and sixties, all its buildings should be respected, especially the Royal Festival Hall, the Hayward Gallery and the Queen Elizabeth Hall which are particularly fine examples of their period.

The public space needs to be defined and designed, and where possible new activities introduced, both public and private, such as schools for music and the arts, workshops, university faculties, postgraduate residences, housing, hotels, offices and shops. Proper streets for cars, buses and pedestrians should run through the area. Links with the neighbouring districts need to be reinforced and especially the connections to the North Bank.

The instrument of design is extremely important to avoid the incompleteness of a master plan and the over determination of architectural proposals. The proper instrument for urban design is the project-plan which goes further than

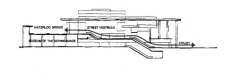

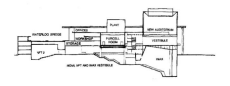

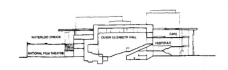

73

OPPOSITE, FROM ABOVE: Plan showing guidelines of urban design concept; plans of ground, vestibule and upper levels; elevation showing, from L to R, Waterloo Bridge, Hungerford Bridge and Westminster Bridge; FROM ABOVE: Section through street vestibule; section through Purcell Room, IMAX and new auditoriums; section through QEH; OVERLEAF: Perspective showing the proposed Juliet Tower, from the north bank

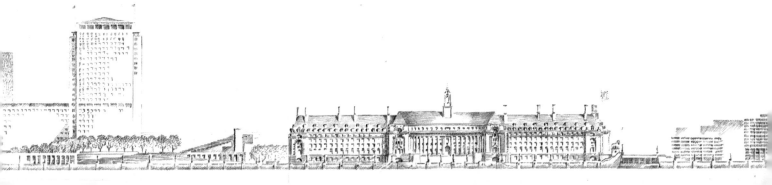

a plan but leaves freedom for architectural expression in the future.

Cultural centres in the twenty first century should lose their exclusiveness and become part of the city structure making cultural activities an integral part of urban life accessible for all, including the casual passer-by.

The Wider Area

After many decades of similar proposals the master plan should meet the challenge of re-establishing a strong pedestrian link between the north and south banks of the River Thames.

It is also important not to miss the unique opportunity offered by the following points:

Firstly, the new Waterloo International Terminal for trains using the Channel Tunnel converts Waterloo Station into London's vestibule to and from European capitals. This calls for the recovery of a grand public square in front of Waterloo Station by restoring the simple street system that existed before, and eliminating the confusion caused by both the barrier of the Hungerford railway viaduct and the traffic roundabout known as the Bull Ring. It should be remembered that a Grand Square was first proposed by John Lacy in 1760 for the South Bank area.

Secondly, the construction of the Jubilee Line extension under the River Thames improves the public transport connections with Waterloo Station, thus providing another opportunity to study the efficiency of the rail link to Charing Cross.

It is proposed to remove this part of the railway, creating a new terminal, Waterloo East, generating maximum efficiency of a single transport interchange: trains, underground and buses. This concentration will generate a high density of business and commercial interests in Lambeth without having to provide for increased private vehicular traffic.

A Light Railway Transport system from Waterloo Station to Charing Cross could establish a shuttle service handling 8,000 passengers an hour with the advantage that it would also be used by passengers from the two existing Waterloo terminals as well as people going specifically to the South Bank Centre. A tall cylindrical office building, forty floors high, together with a

lower rectangular tower on the Elizabeth House site, will regulate the composition of towers around the Grand Square and behind the existing Shell tower. These towers will provide finance for the removal of the Hungerford viaduct, and may well encourage the transfer of offices from the Shell complex to allow redevelopment on these sites as well.

Charing Cross Station has already been converted into a major office and commercial centre. This process could be completed by restoring its historical role as a market and extending it across the renovated Hungerford Bridge in the manner of a new 'London Bridge' with buildings protecting the pedestrian from the adverse climate. The Hungerford Bridge would become a new shopping arcade

similar to Covent Garden making the removal of the railway commercially viable if combined with a new LRT shuttle service.

London, unlike Paris, does not need to reclaim its European role with mega-buildings, but decades of rebuilding the city from the juxtaposition of separate proposals from the private sector alone have eroded its tradition of related public spaces.

The South Bank Centre, by wishing to reconnect with the city, provides a unique opportunity to create two major public spaces – a Grand Square in front of Waterloo Station the size of Trafalgar Square, and a New Mall from this square to Charing Cross across the River Thames.

The loan of Hungerford Bridge for railway transit should now come to an

end and the bridge be used to unite the north and south banks. It is an event that will have an enormous political, economic, cultural and social impact on London.

All access should be from ground level streets avoiding specific segregation of uses and allowing freedom of movement for the future and a higher level of security through mixed usage. 'Cul-de-sacs' between buildings should be eliminated and a street grid established that clearly defines the different areas and allows possible access all round the existing buildings. A two-lane street parallel to the riverside walkway will complete the grid already initiated in front of the RFH, but the 'foyer' between the RFH, the Hayward and QEH would be treated like a square for pedestrians and some vehicles.

Secondly, removal of the brick Hungerford railway viaduct will allow a new mall linking the Grand Square in front of Waterloo Station with Charing Cross and Trafalgar Square. This will in effect create a 'High Street' passing through the South Bank Centre.

Thirdly, the RFH, with the surrounding ground level streets will be freed from the confusion of upper level walkways, except for the riverside terrace. With the removal of the brick Hungerford viaduct the terrace over the service area can be redesigned to accommodate a significant stepped access from the New Mall. The open-air 'foyer' at ground level between the RFH and the Hayward and QEH Arts complex to the north will allow a restoration of the original ground floor entrance of the RFH.

Fourthly, the Hayward Gallery, the QEH, the Purcell Room, the NFT and the MOMI are to be conserved, but enclosed as buildings within an outer building so that all the multiple terraces become interior spaces. This outer building should be designed on the same principles established by Sir Denys Lasdun for the RNT so that they read as a single urban composition split by the Waterloo Bridge. This would establish an 'architectural calming' effect on the existing constructions. These principles are essentially a composition of layers related orthogonally

to the bridge picking up a symmetrical composition of 45° from the centre of Waterloo Bridge with the NT. However the upper roof layer should acquire a form to relate to the RFH and the River Thames.

To provide the most efficient use of the services, terraces, vestibules and provide the maximum amount of alternative cultural offers, both the new auditorium with 475 seats and the Imax cinema should be situated within this new cultural complex. The Imax cinema, not needing natural light, could be sunk into the ground with the new auditorium above. It will also allow direct access to the Imax cinema from the MOMI and NFT.

Fifthly, the Hungerford car-park and the Jubilee Gardens are to be a public park in the form of a shallow bowl and enclosed with splayed walls for wind protection and occasional controlled admittance.

Towards the former County Hall the 'hills' of the park can be altered to accommodate exhibition galleries facing the Thames. The construction of this park should echo the scale and brickwork of Lambeth Palace further up the river to contrast with the white stone of the surrounding buildings.

The architects' aims are essentially to recover a portion of the city south of the river whilst also integrating the relationships of the arts within the area.

RICHARD ROGERS PARTNERSHIP

'To make a city creative you have to get culture out of the museum and into the streets, catch people off guard. You can't just sit back and wait for them to come to you. The Pompidou Centre has taught us that.' (*Jacques Chirac*).

The Richard Rogers Partnership proposals are designed to address the needs of the site itself, its relationship to the immediate neighbourhood and its potential to re-focus the heart of London. To be a success the South Bank must become a destination in its own right, an integral part of the Centre of London.

The proposals are as follows:
• Harness the potential of the South Bank Centre to galvanise its neighbourhood.

• Serve more people by strengthening and unifying a vital area of London.
• Draw together all who pass through, work near, live by or simply visit the South Bank.
• Achieve the correct balance of uses and activities to create the critical mass needed for a self-sustaining, rich and inspiring environment that will thrive into the next century.
• Turn the notion of the arts complex on its head by creating a centre that is open fifteen hours a day, every day, whatever the weather.
• Use the current facilities and spaces to their full potential to create a rich public realm.
• Expand the range of facilities to meet

the demands of changing public expectations of the arts and the changing requirements of the artists.
• Establish the appropriate scale of intervention necessary to achieve the transformation of the South Bank into London's arts quarter.

As originally conceived, the Royal Festival Hall, Queen Elizabeth Hall and Purcell Room provided 'black box' auditoria for the staging of formal events. Performances have a limited time frame covering the period of approximately 7pm until 11pm. Nicholas Snowman observed in his introductory remarks to the competition that audiences for such traditional events are in decline but that attendance of open Foyer events

78

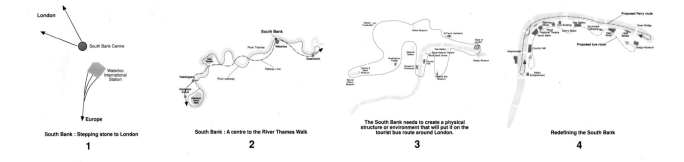

South Bank : Stepping stone to London
1

South Bank : A centre to the River Thames Walk
2

The South Bank needs to create a physical structure or environment that will put it on the tourist bus route around London.
3

Redefining the South Bank
4

continues to grow. Television and the computer, amongst other things, have changed the expectations of audiences both of the arts events themselves and also of ancillary functions such as shops, bars and restaurants. Changing expectations have implications on all aspects of the institution: staging facilities, auditorium, programming, foyer space – exhibition space/performance spaces, support functions, catering and retail.

The RFH by comparison with the QEH/Purcell Room was designed with a large amount of ancillary, front of house space, arranged on many levels within the larger volume defined by the building envelope. In trying to reach out to a younger and wider audience the South Bank has begun to utilise this foyer space for more informal performances and exhibitions, and by a happy coincidence the lobby

spaces provided in the RFH lend themselves to (and indeed encourage) the staging of events.

The RFH model demonstrates a central tenet of the practice's proposals: that an increase in the range of spaces suited for performance and exhibitions will encourage an increase in the range of activities staged.

By contrast the QEH, Purcell Room and Hayward Galleries are enveloped in a series of large open terraces with very little enclosed open house space. These external spaces offer no protection and no degree of enclosure which enables them to be used, either for events or informal activities, in anything but the very best of weathers. They are generally wind-swept, and the English climate is rarely warm enough to allow the external terraces to be used by daytime or evening visitors. The presence of simply a roof 'canopy'

Panoramic bird's-eye view of the new South Bank from the north bank; OVERLEAF, FROM ABOVE L TO R: Plan showing the demolition of a selective amount of the raised walkways to release the ground level around the RFH; plan illustrating the varying degrees of enclosure provided over the remaining raised terraces, walkways and the embankment to recapture these lost spaces; plan showing the arrangement of a mix of activities within these enclosures to create an all day, every day centre of activity; plan showing renewed clarity and transparency of the buildings and open spaces; plan of the re-integration of the circulation routes on the site with the movement patterns of the neighbouring areas, thereby increasing accessibility; plan demonstrating the reconciliation of service access requirements on the Upper Ground/Belvedere Road with pedestrian circulation thereby establishing an address for the South Bank in Lambeth; section illustrating the flow of space from one building to the next

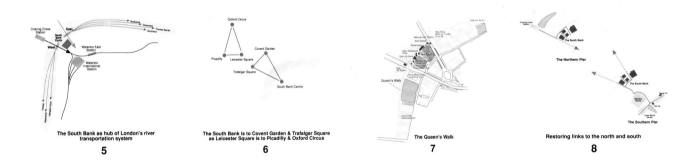

The South Bank as hub of London's river transportation system

5

The South Bank is to Covent Garden & Trafalgar Square as Leicester Square is to Picadilly & Oxford Circus

6

The Queen's Walk

7

Restoring links to the north and south

8

would mean that hospitable conditions will prevail more frequently.

The proposals to re-invigorate the South Bank can be divided into four distinct elements. An order of implementation has been suggested but they can be phased to suit funding arrangements and the centre's own requirements.

The Crystal Palace

The existing structures of the QEH, Purcell Room and Hayward Gallery are enclosed by a roof which acts as an environmental canopy, recapturing the under-utilised terraces and creating a new series of public spaces. The roof also establishes a unified architectural expression of the disparate elements that constitute the South Bank. This simple act dramatically increases the amount of accommodation available without major new construction.

The roof canopy is conceived as a series of interlocking 'scales', whose structure can adapt to the profile of the buildings beneath. It will create a temperate micro-climate, with shelter from rain and protection from wind, capable of modifying the environment in a number of different ways. It will have an organic quality of selective permeability to daylight and air: the temperate space beneath is daylit and can 'breathe'. The construction of the roof can be carried out incrementally.

In addition to exhibition spaces and a lecture theatre the Crystal Palace will contain an informal (free access) exhibition and performance space, museum shops, book shops, a video library, bars, cafes and restaurants.

A formal entry to the Crystal Palace will be established on Upper Ground/Belvedere Road. A less formal entry will also be established on the river front. Between these a main thoroughfare will be established giving access to the major functions and spaces within the Crystal Palace. A central ticket office is proposed adjacent to the esplanade. A large canopied space will offer pro-

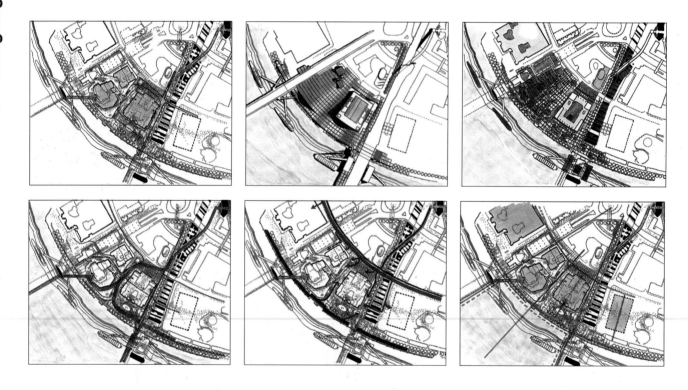

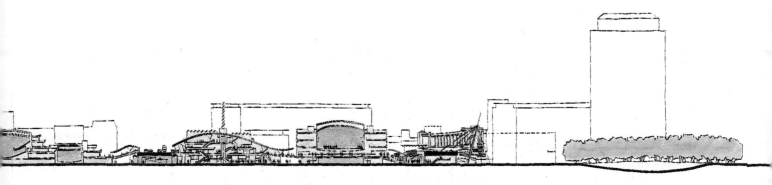

tection to pedestrians queuing in the plaza. Cafes will be located around this plaza. The glazed facade alongside the linking spine will be animated by the pedestrian. Views will be afforded of the activities within the Crystal Palace from outside.

New Arrangements for the Royal Festival Hall

The raised walkway around the RFH will be demolished, releasing the building so that it stands freely within a cathedral close-like setting.

The road alongside the railway arches will be opened up, planted with an avenue of trees and re-paved for pedestrian use. Restaurants and bars will be relocated under the arches, extended with glass conservatories to create a 'restaurant row' overlooking the RFH.

A grand forecourt on Upper Ground will act as a formal drop-off entry for the RFH and Crystal Palace. Similar to a paved market square, the forecourt will re-connect the RFH and the rest of the South Bank with the neighbourhood by forming a public focus.

A new auditorium will be located below ground, similar to the auditorium at IRCAM in Paris, between the RFH and the river bank. Access will be from a new entry pavilion, a glazed struc-

FROM ABOVE L TO R: The new enclosure enables the empty terraces to be re-occupied; the central ticket office, set at the heart of the site, will be animated by people queuing for same-day tickets; entrance to the Hayward Gallery, QEH, Purcell Room, MOMI and NFT will all be arranged within the Crystal Palace; the forecourt establishes a formal setting for the RFH; an outdoor arena is planned above the new auditorium; the South Bank eyots will animate the river basin with activity; cross section showing how the South Bank will be reconnected with areas to the north and south; OVERLEAF: Thames elevation

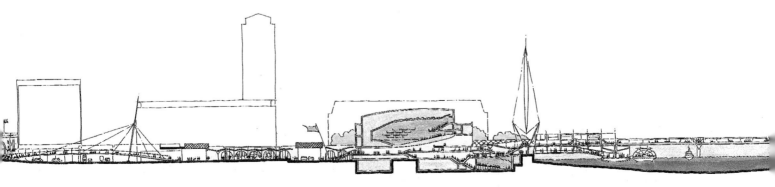

ture admitting light to the lobby below, and containing lifts, stairs and escalators. It will be a similar structure to the pyramid at the Louvre.

The roof of the new auditorium will form a bandstand arena at ground level. This will be partially enclosed, with canopy and walls, adjustable to suit conditions. The roofscape of the new auditorium comprising outdoor arena, entry pavilion and the riverside walk extend the foyer space of the RFH outward to the river front.

Connections

The South Bank could be described as an island which needs to be linked back to the mainland with a pier, both the north and south. To encourage movement to and through the site links to the adjoining neighbourhoods will be upgraded by strengthening the two key bridge connections, Hungerford Bridge and the route to Waterloo station.

A new bridge connection springing from the concourse level in the Victory Arch of Waterloo Station is proposed that would cross York Road and bring the pedestrian to ground level in a gentle moving curve. This would also serve to link the centre to the Old Vic and market beyond.

The Hungerford railway bridge pedestrian way will be replaced by a wide new passerelle. Escalators replace stairs, better oriented to link the South Bank with the foot of Villiers Street. Escalators will also connect the bridge to the embankment, an important drop-off point for tourist buses, and at the South Bank end. Similar connections at the bridgeheads are proposed for the Waterloo Road bridge. Travelators in the Hungerford Bridge Passerelle will carry pedestrians across the river and take advantage of the wide vistas of the city. These will create an attraction similar to the experience of the escalators at the Pompidou Centre.

The South Bank overlooks a tremendous body of water, contained within the two bridges and on a gracious curve in the river. Views out over this basin are diminished by the current location of the river pontoon. In place of this two major floating islands or

eyots are proposed, one under each of the bridges. The eyots are intended as floating villages giving life and interest to the sides of the South Bank Basin. Boatels could be moored at the eyots providing student accommodation for term time and hostel accommodation during the holidays. Floating restaurants and swimming pools could also be moored here.

The Thames is under-used as a transportation route. An expanded system of boats could utilise the eyots as the main London Terminal with commuter services west to Putney and east to the Docklands, as well as pleasure trips servicing further afield. With easy access to three major railway stations and three underground stations the South Bank eyots would be well placed to become the hub of an integrated river transportation system.

The Queen's Walk

To extend the usability of this important external urban space for all weather use an esplanade is proposed. The esplanade precipitates the creation of a series of spaces for retail, arts and many other informal uses. The new Queen's Walk will be protected by glass screens to create an esplanade, continuing in the tradition of the English seaside pier, which is suited to the climate. Night-time lighting will attract visitors to the walkway which serves to unify the arts complexes along the South Bank. This gives much greater flexibility in the programming and marketing the notion of the arts district and the separate components. Some of the activities that might be located along the Queen's Walk include a market place; cafes; virtual reality show; book stalls; a student art gallery; informal performance spaces; a London forum for the Open University

The proposed phasing suggests one way of re-invigorating the South Bank. If the strategy is successful it will become a significant magnet to people and consequently new activities. By strengthening connections the South Bank will be transformed into the heart of a cultural district which draws people to it and then to the myriad of cultural activities on offer.

TROUGHTON MCASLAN

Destination

The South Bank can become part of London. An inevitable part of London, to which one naturally gravitates, without having to be equipped as if for an expedition. It can become a part of London which is known not merely for its temples of high culture – it has several of those already, and will have more – but as a place with a distinct character, the kind of quarter that cannot easily be created from scratch, but which, over the years, is pieced together. Over 40 years, one element to another has been added at the South Bank. Now, the task is to take those pieces, and augment and transform them into an apparently effortless whole.

The interventions we propose to make to the South Bank may be likened to certain aspects of horticulture. We intend to prune hard in certain areas, to graft new additions on to others, to introduce fresh stock selectively, and to open up vistas and connections with the surrounding landscape. We see the involvement of surrounding interests and landowners, and close collaboration with leading artists, as important.

Arrival

An essential part of our master-planning approach is to make the South Bank readily and naturally accessible from all sides, and to set up better routes through the site from front to back. Approaching from the Embankment, we treat the South Bank as if it were a portion of the 'lost' north bank. The Centre is signalled by light towers flanking both Hungerford and Waterloo Bridges to provide generous access, by the lit volume of the new riverboat peninsula and Wintergarden behind, and by a programme of light-based artworks picking out all the separate built elements of the arts quarter. Access is by a widened, part-glazed Hungerford footbridge and by a complementary sheltered access across Waterloo Bridge.

From Waterloo, in conjunction with much-needed traffic calming and pedestrian priority measures, an important new direct diagonal connection is made across York Road through to a new pedestrian piazza at the rear of the Royal Festival Hall. This point of arrival is marked by a reconstructed 'Skylon', signifying the importance of what is currently a virtually ignored hinterland. From here, you can move naturally either to the Royal Festival Hall straight ahead, to the shops and stalls of a new Hungerford Bridge Market on your left, or to the Wintergarden on your right.

Wintergarden

The Wintergarden concept is central to this approach. As part of the urbanising process, the architects want to reinforce links between the Waterloo hinterland and the river, and they also want to provide adaptable, non-intrusive forms of shelter in the open areas of the site. The Wintergarden does both. Troughton McAslan envisage several others in the greater South Bank area, sited in the ' slots' between the riverside buildings, acting as semi-open spaces and responsive to the climate.

The first and most important Wintergarden is at the exact heart of our masterplanning proposal. At this point – the 'slot' between the Royal Festival Hall and the later buildings of the

Queen Elizabeth Hall and the Hayward Gallery a delicate high-level transparent canopy is introduced. It spans the space but does not seal it, opens to the air on fine summer days and closes to create shelter in bad weather. It runs from a new vehicle drop-off point on Belvedere Road, and rises to terrace level at the front. Its axis continues to form a new promontory, an intriguing circular peninsula in the river acting as pier, moorings and restaurant.

The floor of the Wintergarden is created at ground level by the selective removal of upper-level walkways and the replacement of the present service road by a new secure service access and covered loading/unloading dock off Belvedere Road by the Waterloo Bridge approach. The Wintergarden with its indoor/outdoor feel, its trees and fountains, shops and cafes, also provides the key access point to the RFH, QEH, Purcell Room, Hayward Gallery and – as explained next, the new medium-sized auditorium. It thus

becomes a very animated, dynamic space, a place to meet and eat, a natural and desirable focus for activities in this area of the South Bank.

A family of related wintergardens moderating the spaces between Waterloo Bridge and the Royal National Theatre, between the Royal National Theatre and the IBM building, between IBM and London Weekend Television, is envisaged. These, unlike the principal Wintergarden described above, will allow controlled access to service vehicles.

New Auditorium

The introduction of the new 475-seat chamber music auditorium is a further important element in the urbanising of the South Bank. The first site was rejected for this was the present Hungerford car park. It is strongly felt that the new auditorium should be close to all three existing music venues, not separated from them, out on a limb. The planning difficulties of placing a building on the Hungerford

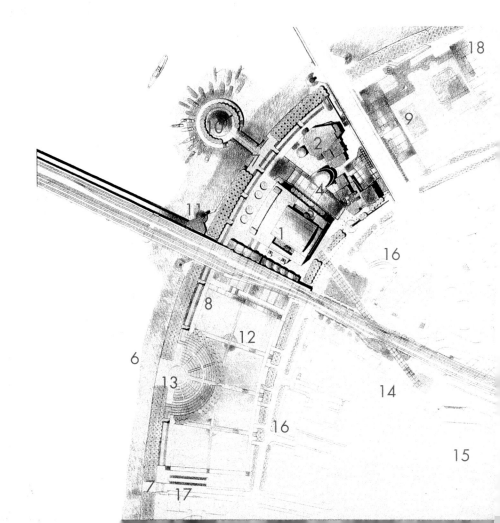

OPPOSITE: 'Festival' perspective; RIGHT: proposed master plan. Key: 1 RFH; 2 QEH; 3 Hayward Gallery; 4 Auditorium; 5 Wintergarden; 6 Queen's Walk; 7 Great Stair; 8 Hungerford Bridge Market; 9 Royal National Theatre; 10 Festival Pier; 11 Bridge Tower; 12 Jubilee Gardens (car park/coach park below); 13 Amphitheatre; 14 Pedestrian Link; 15 Waterloo Station; 16 Shell Centre; 17 County Hall; 18 IBM

15

site, plus the need to integrate it with a car park, plus the proximity of the Jubilee Line working site, are not insuperable problems; but that is not the point. The new auditorium can perform a civilising role in the creation of a new heart to the arts complex. It is accordingly placed as a discrete, clearly recognisable and elegant ovoid form, positioned between the Queen Elizabeth Hall and Hayward Gallery, and emerging into the Wintergarden to face the re-established side entrance of the Royal Festival Hall.

This auditorium – acoustically a 'double box within an egg' – sets up a dialogue between all the main elements of the site. Its form is designed to resolve the complexities of the site geometry on the 'fault-line' between the RFH alignment and the differing alignment of the later buildings. Similarly it is a form that reconciles the changes of level at this point and provides a visual hub to the whole. By sharing new foyer space with the upgraded QEH,

Purcell Room and Hayward Gallery, it also acts as a circulation focus. The masterplan provides the flexibility for the new auditorium to be built in either early or late phases of the programme.

The Great Stair
The level differences throughout the site are tackled in two ways. Firstly, high-level walkways around the RFH are removed while most of those of the Hayward/QEH complex on the far side of the Wintergarden are retained and improved. The exception here is the riverside terrace of the QEH, which is cut back. Better vertical access is provided – most notably by punching through to link the ground, terrace and upper (now with restaurant) terrace levels of the enhanced QEH foyer.

Secondly, level changes between all the buildings and the riverside are resolved in one strong gesture: a new 'Great Stair', which sweeps around the whole frontage from Waterloo Bridge to County Hall, regularly pierced with

arena-like access slots to ground-level activities behind. It is not merely a visual device but a landscaped, human-scale stair, subtly incorporating ramps for the disabled. It will also be a very popular place for people to meet and sit to gaze across the river. On the Jubilee Gardens site, the Great Stair curves inwards to form a riverside amphitheatre.

The Hungerford Bridge Market
While the Wintergarden will provide a home for many of the retail activities currently cluttering the Royal Festival Hall, many others will be accommodated in a substantial shopping street based on the Hungerford Bridge railway arches. The arched units will extend out either side of the viaduct, animating this flank of the Festival Hall. On the Hungerford car park side, a row of freestanding pavilions will face the extended-arch units to form a balancing street. The market will run from York Road to the riverside walk.

FROM ABOVE, L TO R: Existing problem of severe pedestrian/vehicular conflict; proposed vehicular movement and servicing rationalised and removed from *the core site, with conflict minimised; existing setting has little sense of place; proposed interventions will create a focus for the South Bank; existing exposed* *environment with wind funnelling through buildings creates uncomfortable conditions; proposed landscape and Wintergarden will modify and improve environ-* *mental conditions; existing context is inhospitable, and lacks adequate linkages; proposed strategy will enhance setting and amenities and forge new linkages*

Towards County Hall

The Hungerford car park/Jubilee Gardens site becomes a complete new semi-formal garden, raised above car and coach parking to the terrace level at the top of the Great Stair – thus providing a unifying level throughout the front of the site. This is the opportunity for a significant landscaping exercise where an arrangement of small, even intimate planted spaces builds up to an urban scale. The gardens are to carry medium-weight structures and will serve as the main site for the Millennium Festival of 2001, and for various informal pavilions and kiosks as demand suggests.

The riverside amphitheatre – its semi-circular form balancing the outward curve of the riverboat promontory on the downriver side of the bridge – enjoys the unrivalled backdrop of the City and Westminster skyline. The 3,000 seat amphitheatre and gardens will become a permanent focus of open-air events such as concerts, dance events, recitals and parades. Skateboarders need look no further.

Royal Festival Hall Improvements

Making retail space in the Wintergarden and the Hungerford Bridge Market means that the temple of the big concert hall can be cleansed of its jumble of food outlets and shops. Its transparency is re-gained, and its side and rear entrances re-opened, involving the removal of a small later back addition. It becomes once more a dignified and welcoming public place.

Hayward Gallery /Queen Elizabeth Hall Improvements

The Hayward Gallery will have a new shared foyer at ground level in the Wintergarden, better direct access from Waterloo Bridge, and will enjoy additional gallery and public space in a glass-skinned volumetric extension next to the Bridge. Backstage and front-of house facilities at the QEH and Purcell Room are improved to bring them up to the standard of the new auditorium alongside.

The entrance to the Museum of the Moving Image is moved to the riverfront: in time MOMI could relate to a second Wintergarden between Waterloo Bridge and the Royal National Theatre.

These are the main elements of the masterplan, described in more detail in the 'Information' section at the back of this proposal. It is proposed to divide the works in five fundable phases through to the year 2001: all are highly realistic, buildable, and sustainable in terms of running costs and revenue. The proposal to introduce proceedings with a pilot 'light sculpture' has also been approached.

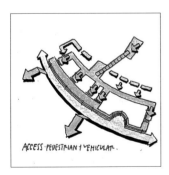

ACCESS·PEDESTRIAN + VEHICULAR·

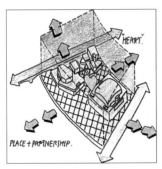

PLACE + PARTNERSHIP·

LANDSCAPE AND ENVIRONMENT

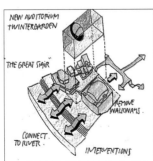

NEW AUDITORIUM + WINTERGARDEN

THE GREAT STAIR

REMOVE WALKWAYS·

CONNECT TO RIVER·

INTERVENTIONS

Colour sketches of light sculpture – the tide's ebbing cycle begins

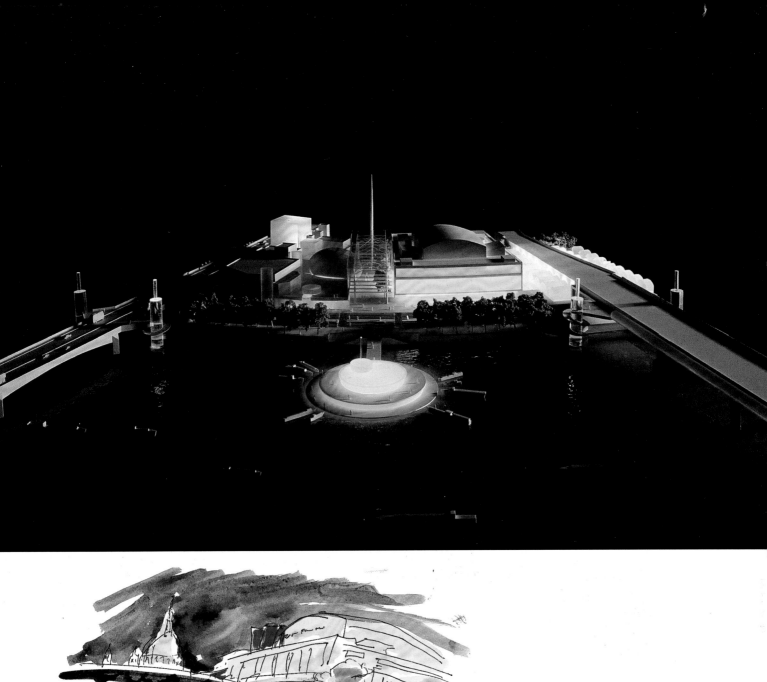

THE FINALISTS
ALLIES AND MORRISON ARCHITECTS

The emphasis of the three principal goals reinforces the continuity of the second stage entry. The architects re-state their intention to re-establish the South Bank Centre in its wider context, creating a strong sense of unity for the Centre and maximising the use of the existing buildings.

For a variety of reasons, the Centre has remained isolated from its immediate surroundings. This proposal establishes a new main entrance to the Royal Festival Hall, and to the Centre as a whole, on Belvedere Road, facing onto a new public square.

The second objective is to provide the Centre with a strong sense of unity. Although it exists as a disparate group of buildings, it has a common management and common artistic goals. The architects have therefore placed particular importance on the need to transform the relationship between the individual buildings by connecting the foyers of these buildings with a major external pedestrian space, raised above a new shared foyer at ground level.

The third objective is to exploit the full potential of the existing buildings. The Queen Elizabeth Hall and the Hayward Gallery are major public resources which, with extension and adjustment, could become both more welcoming and more effective. This proposal inserts a metal and glass armature containing new facilities, new circulation and new entrances.

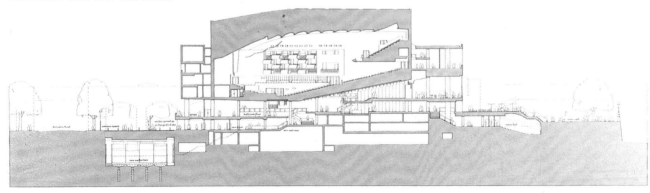

OPPOSITE, FROM ABOVE: Perspective showing new main entrance to the Royal Festival Hall from Belvedere Road; section showing proposed relationship of main terrace to the river; LEFT: Overall perspective; FROM ABOVE: Site Plan; upper level and intermediate level plans; ground level and main foyer level plans; section showing new piazza, the shared lower foyer and the new entrance to the Hayward Gallery

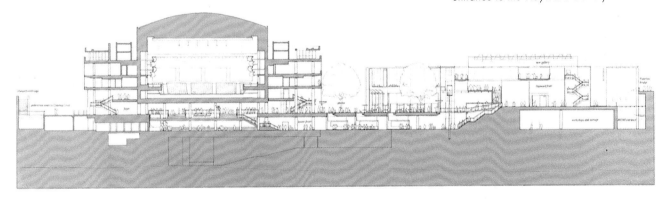

MICHAEL HOPKINS AND PARTNERS

This proposal allows the existing architecture to breathe. The addition of a transparent roof and the clearing of walkways will ensure it becomes an exciting innovative statement for the new millennium. Working from the complex existing structure, a realistically achievable strategy for regeneration is suggested – 'We shall invent an architecture which understands what the earlier generation was trying to achieve and then adjust it, but with one clear change of emphasis. We want to get people back to ground level.'

One of the key issues in the scheme is the provision of a 'Central Avenue' which is the main urban space and primary link between the arts buildings and Riverside Walk. A central canopy will provide shelter and focus for outdoor events. The Royal Festival Hall is once again revealed as an uncluttered, freestanding building with its original entrance restored. By establishing the ground level throughout, complete access is available to the disabled.

A central feature of this proposal is the reappearance of a tower on the site. Instead of the previously suggested Skylon Tower, this scheme promotes a new structure that will become London's equivalent of the Eiffel Tower. It will be a symbol of the South Bank, just as its predecessor was in 1951, but this time marking an even more important milestone – the new millennium. Positioned in the Thames with boat moorings around its base, this feature will be an attraction in its own right with public restaurants and a viewing platform.

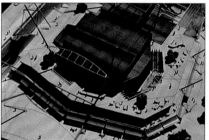

ABOVE: The South Bank at the millennium; CENTRE L TO R: Model view across the Thames; model view of upper terrace with roof removed; Millennium Tower; the Central Avenue; Millennium Tower from Central Avenue; BELOW L TO R: Model view from the Thames; model view of Winter Garden roof; view from upper terrace; Hayward Gallery foyer; the new upper foyer bar

92

RICHARD ROGERS PARTNERSHIP

For this second stage submission the architects provide a confirmation, reiteration and development of their original objectives.

The main initial objective was to double the number of people who visit the South Bank Centre by making the South Bank visible from the north bank, providing easier access, creating a comfortable environment all year round and ensuring that the area becomes both a place to see and be seen.

Broadly speaking, the development for this stage concentrates on two themes: firstly, technical issues relating to service access, disabled access, environmental conditions, construction and construction costs, maintenance and running costs; secondly, spatial issues relating to the nature of the spaces defined by the canopies, specifically by the Crystal Palace enclosure and the Queen's Walk canopy.

The unification of the site by the act of enclosure achieves many of the desired parameters. It creates sufficient floor space to provide not only the accommodation required in the brief but it also provides extra space which has been allocated for a new entrance hall, an area for restaurants offering spectacular views, a zone for retail along the river's edge and a good service area to all these facilities. In addition it will also be economical to run with strict environmental controls which extend the economic life of the existing structures as well as reducing their energy requirements with the establishment of a buffer zone, dramatically improving economic efficiency.

Overall this scheme intends to create a desirable and stunning place to be throughout the entire year. The impact of enclosure on the environmental conditions guarantees clement surroundings which can be maintained for the user regardless of the weather.

BELOW: Sections and plans; OPPOSITE: Perspective from within the Crystal Palace

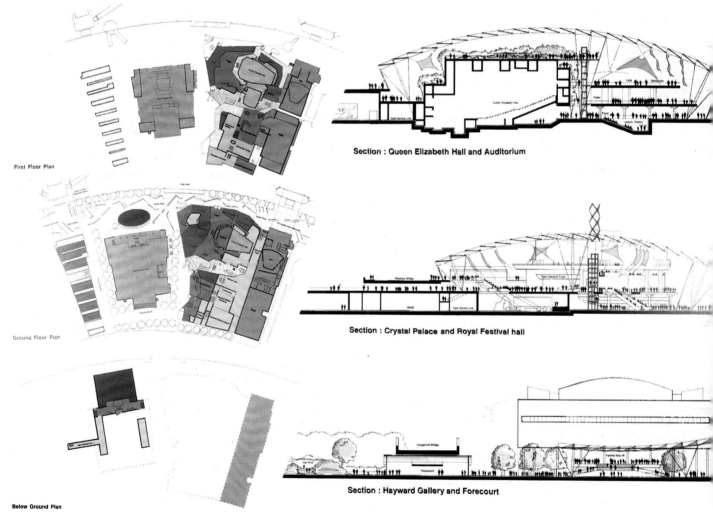

First Floor Plan

Ground Floor Plan

Below Ground Plan

Section : Queen Elizabeth Hall and Auditorium

Section : Crystal Palace and Royal Festival hall

Section : Hayward Gallery and Forecourt

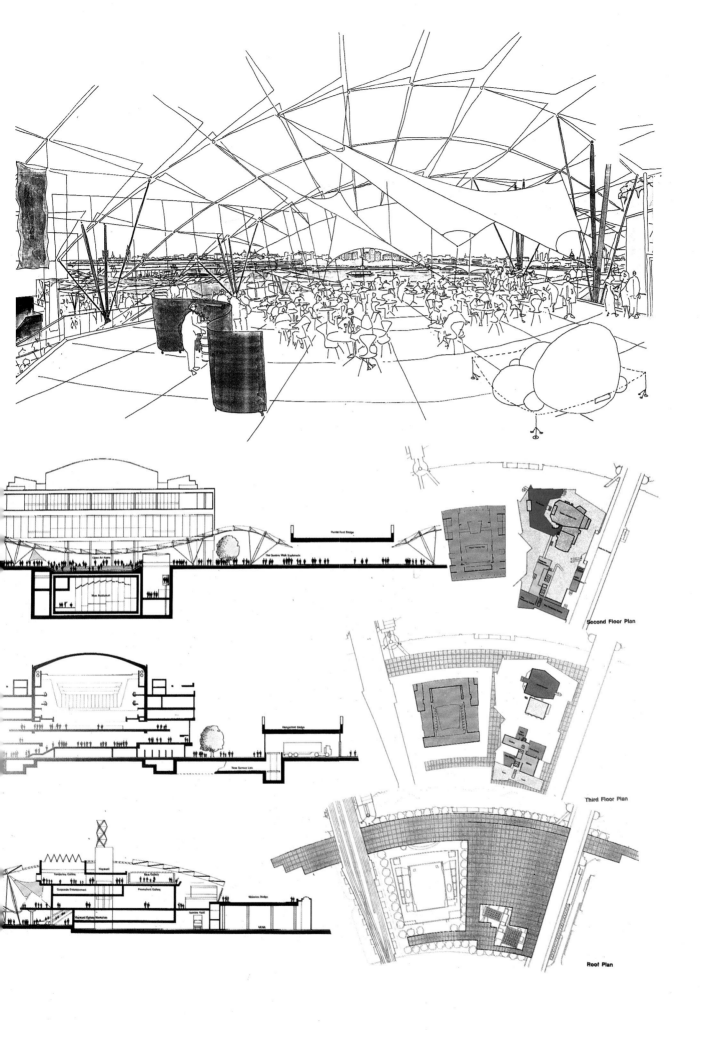

Second Floor Plan

Third Floor Plan

Roof Plan

ASSESSORS FOR THE ARCHITECTURAL MASTER PLANNER

The panel of eight assessors who were responsible for selecting the master planner for the South Bank Centre site is listed below. The team was chaired by Sir Brian Corby, Chairman of the South Bank Centre and was assisted in its work by Gordon Graham CBE PPRIBA, the Centre's Architectural Advisor for the redevelopment plans.

Sir Brian Corby Chairman and formerly Chief Executive of the Prudential Corporation. Former Director of the Bank of England and former President of the Confederation of British Industry.

Eldred Evans Architect and partner of Evans and Shalev, London. She has had a long and distinguished career in private practice since 1962 and extensive experience of architectural competitions, both as assessor and competitor. Her recent projects include the new Tate Gallery at St Ives and Truro Crown Courts.

Anish Kapoor Artist and sculptor. He has exhibited extensively both in the UK and abroad. Recent one-person exhibitions include *Anish Kapoor drawings* at the Tate Gallery 1990-91 and a show at the Lisson Gallery, 1993. He represented Britain at the Venice Biennale in 1990 where he was awarded the Premio Duemila, and won the Turner Prize in 1991.

Henry Meyric Hughes Director of Exhibitions at the South Bank Centre and previously Head of Visual Arts at the British Council. He was British Commissioner for five editions of the Venice Biennale, including the exhibition. *British Architecture Today: Six Protagonists* in 1991.

Christian de Portzamparc One of France's most prolific and respected architects with a very wide range of experience, from urban housing to architectural interiors. Over the past decade, he has been involved in a series of competition projects devoted to music and the arts: the Dance School of the Paris Opera, the Bastille Opera and the City of Music in Paris which included a music conservatory, museum and auditorium.

Martin Smith South Bank Board member, Managing Partner of Phoenix Securities, and Chairman of the Orchestra of the Age of Enlightenment.

Nicholas Snowman Chief Executive of the South Bank Centre and previously General Director (Arts) 1986-92. Artistic Director of IRCAM at the Pompidou Centre in Paris 1972-86. Co-founder of the London Sinfonietta and Ensemble Inter-Contemporain.

Alan Stanton Partner in Stanton Williams Architects. Current projects include an extension for the Ashmolean Museum in Oxford and the refurbishment of Compton Verney House as an art centre. On the South Bank, Stanton Williams are consultant architects to the Royal National Theatre and have designed many of the major exhibitions at the Hayward Gallery.

SYMPOSIUM PARTICIPANTS

Chaired by Paul Finch, *Architect's Journal*, and Robert Maxwell, *Architect*

Marina Adams *Landscape Architect* • Susie Allen *Royal College of Art* • Richard Balfe *MEP* • Val Bourne *Dance Umbrella* • Peter Brades *Barefoot, Brades & Fanning* • Susan Brades *South Bank Centre* • Roger Bloom • Geoffrey Broadbent *Architect* • Jake Brown *Architect* • Lucy Bullivant • Richard Burdett *The Architecture Foundation* • Esther Caplin *Vision for London* • Gerry Carter *Environmental Consulting Office* • Rory Coonan *Arts Council of England* • Michael Compton *Art Historian* • Trevor Dannatt *Architect* • Ian Davidson *Lifschutz Davidson* • Maurice Dowdall *Environmental Consulting Office* • Professor David Dunster *South Bank University* • Rose Fenton *LIFT* • Richard Fleming *MacCormac Jamieson Prichard* • Catherine Graham-Harrison *Tate Gallery* • Ian Gerney *Government Office of London* • Malcolm Haxby *Westminster City Council* • Louis Hellman *Architect* • Kate Heron *Architect* • Noel Hill *RIBA London Region* • Gavin Hogbin *University of Cambridge* • Sarah Hopkins *The Architectural Foundation* • Caryl Hubbard • David Hutchinson *London Research Centre* • Nicola Johnston *Westminster City Council* • Alex Lifschutz *Lifschutz Davidson* • Richard MacCormac *MacCormac Jamieson Prichard* • Emma Mandley *London Television Centre* • Richard Matthews *Environmental Consulting Office* • Claire Melhuish *Building Design* • John Melvin *Architect* • Jeremy Melvin *Building Design* • Henry Meyric Hughes *South Bank Centre* • Lucy Neil *LIFT* • Anne Page *London Research Centre* • Lucy Payne *BBC TV* • John Phillipps *Llewelyn-Davies* • Alex Ritchie *Imagination* • Martin Reynolds *Imagination* • John Rowland • Julia Rowntree *LIFT* • Edwina Sassoon *Arts Consultant* • Nicholas Snowman *Chief Executive South Bank Centre* • Colin Stanbridge *Carlton Television* • Charles Summers *Shell International* • John Taylor *BURA (British Urban Regeneration)* • Huw Thomas *Sir Norman Foster and Partners* • Maggie Toy *Architectural Design* • Iain Tuckett *Coin Street Community Builders* • Ian Turkington *Whitelaw Turkington* • Marina Vaizey *National Art Collections Fund* • Abigail Warren *LPAC* • John Welsh *Building Design* • Trisha Williams *Coin Street Community Builders* • Professor Colin St John Wilson *Architect* • Ewart Wooldridge *South Bank Centre* • Freda Wooldridge *The Friedland Group* • Maggie Whitlum *Royal National Theatre* • Meloneze Wynter *London Borough of Southwark*